D0717516

INSTANT DOG TRAINING

CLAIRE ARROWSMITH

The Quick Response Programme

INTERPET PUBLISHING

CREDITS

Published by
Interpet Publishing,
Vincent Lane,
Dorking,
Surrey RH4 3YX,
England

© 2011 Interpet Publishing
    Ltd.
All rights reserved

ISBN 978-1-84286-231-5

Editor: Philip de Ste. Croix
Designer: Philip Clucas MCDS
Photographer: Roddy Paine
Production management:
    Consortium, Suffolk
Print production: 1010 Printing
    International Ltd, China

Disclaimer
The information and
recommendations in this book
are given without any
guarantees on behalf of the
author and publisher, who
disclaim any liability with the
use of this material.

Author's Note
The instant training techniques
described in this book are
suitable for all dogs, but for
the sake of brevity I have
chosen to describe
participating dogs as male
throughout the descriptions
used in the book. This is
purely to simplify the text and
does not imply that any of the
methods are not suitable for
female dogs.

CONTENTS

INTRODUCTION pages 8-13

CHAPTER 1

UNDERSTANDING YOUR DOG

This chapter explains how to interpret a dog's body
language and how to use this insight to improve your
own communication during training **pages 14-23**

CHAPTER 2

GET READY FOR INSTANT TRAINING

Being prepared is central to achieving success with your
training. The principles of **instant** training are explained here
– good timing, consistency, and instant rewards
– and the use of a clicker is described.
Tips and 'what ifs?' also help with
troubleshooting **pages 24-35**

CHAPTER 3

PUPPY TRAINING – SOCIALISING

A young puppy comes into your home almost like a
blank canvas – those first few weeks of life with you
are vital for introducing him to important habituation
and socialisation experiences – meeting other people
and animals, encountering routine household objects,
driving with you in the car – and beginning the first
training exercises **pages 36-39**

'Focus on getting you

timing right...be quick with your rewards!'

Contents continued ▶ ▶ ▶

CONTENTS

'You can work on training your dog

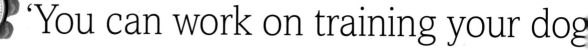

CHAPTER 10 TRAINING FOR WHEN VISITORS CALL

Visitors are not going to enjoy it if your dog hurls himself at the door when the bell rings and then jumps all over them when they enter the house. Here's how to train good manners when people come to call **pages 88-89**

CHAPTER 11 TRAINING AT MEALTIMES

Aggression shown by a dog around his food bowl is quite a common problem that must be addressed. Learn how to teach him better table manners through **instant** training **pages 90-91**

CHAPTER 12 END OF THE DAY

Even as the day draws to a close and everyone gets ready for bed, opportunities for **instant** training present themselves **pages 92-93**

ven when sitting down and relaxing.'

5

With just a little preparation, my advice can be applied

FOREWORD

The guidance that I provide in this book is derived from more than ten years of working as a dog behaviourist. It focuses on some of the most common daily training queries that I am asked. This book about **Instant Dog Training** will NOT transform your dog instantaneously into a perfectly behaved, impeccably trained pet. Just as you took time to learn to read and to achieve all the skills you now have at this stage of your life, your dog also needs time and experience to learn how to behave well.

However, this book will sharpen up your training skills so you learn the importance of being

'**Instant**' when you respond to your dog.

'**Instant**' when you deliver a reward for correct behaviour, and

'**Instant**' when you snatch moments out of your daily routine to practise some quick but rewarding training that will stimulate your dog and help to build his confidence.

nstantly'. If used consistently, you should see rapid results.

INTRODUCTION

Although trainers and behaviourists are often called on to wave their magic wands over badly behaved pets, the reality is that there is no substitute for time and dedication when it comes to training your dog really effectively.

Many people are shocked at how much commitment owning a dog actually entails. A puppy is often expected to arrive, do a few (not too many) naughty puppy activities and then settle straight into family life like the dogs portrayed in old movies. Puppy and dog training is still often seen as an activity only for very keen dog owners and those wanting to go on to compete in obedience or even to show. This is absolutely wrong; dog training is a must for each and every single person who takes on

Right: 'Sit'. It is never too early to start training when a new puppy arrives in the home. However, remember that puppies are liable to tire easily so keep the sessions quite brief.

a dog. No matter what prior experience you have of owning dogs, each new pet has his or her own requirements and idiosyncrasies and you are going to have to spend time discovering what this particular dog's strengths and weaknesses are. There are plenty of caring dog owners with lots of previous experience who find that their newest canine has problems. Training your dog and encouraging desirable behaviour will help to reduce the number of problem dogs in our communities, but of course it is also directly to help you. Being an owner does not mean you're also getting maximum possible enjoyment from the experience. If you don't try to understand your pet and to encourage the best behaviour from him or her, you will never know what your dog has to offer.

Left: Well-trained dogs are a real delight to own – they add a rich extra dimension to our everyday lives.

Dog training is a must for each and every single person who takes on a dog as part of the family

Above: It is an idyllic vision of family life – mother, father, daughter and faithful dog enjoying a day out in the countryside. But it doesn't come ready-made – a dog must be trained to fit in to the family unit.

Above: Dogs do not express affection by hugging one another, so understandably some find that this behaviour causes them anxiety.

It is very easy to buy a dog, yet he or she is possibly the most complex purchase you will ever make. This animal has a personality, instincts, physical and emotional needs, different life stages which alter its needs, and of course the potential to create a great deal of physical harm, emotional upset and expense if things go wrong. Unfortunately things can go wrong and many loving owners find themselves seeking behavioural support, giving up their pets

or even having to choose euthanasia of their pet in very extreme cases. Many of these dogs were unintentionally set up to fail. Poor breeding, lack of early socialisation, inconsistent training and overly high expectations all create the potential for problems. In addition, owners who don't recognise the differences between normal canine and human behaviours may accidentally create problems. For example, humans (and chimpanzees) love to express our devotion by hugging and squeezing babies, family members and friends. Dogs never interact with one another like this and may interpret this behaviour as a threat. Other owners try the natural act of consolation and petting when they see their pet behaving in an anxious way. Unfortunately, dogs don't understand the meaning of this demonstration of affection and the owner may actually be inadvertently reinforcing the fear reaction.

Below: It is sensible to join a training class when you get a new dog, even if you are an experienced owner with many previous dogs to your name. Every dog has its idiosyncrasies and needs individual training.

INTRODUCTION

Above: A dog's brain does not work exactly like a human's; to be a successful trainer you have to develop a sense of how dogs think and react.

Your Dog's Brain

Dogs don't need the same kind of brain function as we do to live their lives. They don't need to plan ahead or consider the past in order to survive. They make associations as they go along and this influences how they behave when they next encounter a similar event or environment.

Of course your dog certainly does have memories and powers of recall; after all you don't need to teach him his name every day and a well-trained dog continues to respond to specific cues throughout his life. A combination of information picked up by your dog's various senses will create associations which form 'memories'. When he picks up those familiar signals again it will trigger off a positive or negative memory association.

Some people believe that their dog is not intelligent because the training they are pursuing takes time to achieve. This may be due to a number of factors including lack of consistency on the part of the trainer. Also bear in mind that the lessons you are trying to teach your dog are probably not actions that he would naturally perform. For example, it is not a natural canine behaviour to sit at every kerb or before greeting another individual. This is taught by building the association between that action in those circumstances and a reward.

Above: Dogs certainly have memories – they can recognise the postman's approach and remember that this means letters at the door.

Above and below: Dogs do not sit down when they greet one another. If we want them routinely to 'Sit', we have to train this using treats.

These two dogs will stand and sniff one another when they choose to meet.

Like us, dogs remember important events more readily than insignificant ones. This is a natural process which helps to keep them safe by making scary events or extremely enjoyable ones stand out. So just because your dog doesn't remember the training command immediately, this does not mean he is not intelligent or has a bad memory; he

Above: Throughout this book I emphasise the benefits of training with a clicker which allows you to mark good behaviour with a 'click'.

simply needs more repetition or a very exciting reward to make the session stand out for him and be recalled the next time.

Timing Is Everything You will need to employ repetition in order for your dog to make the associations necessary to alter his responses. The timing of your reward, or reinforcement, is critical. If your dog is rewarded while he is performing the desirable action, then it is very likely that he will develop a strong association with that response and want to do it again. To help you to pinpoint the moment that you wish to encourage, we will use and discuss clicker training throughout this book. By pairing up the reward and the sound of the clicker you will be able to signal efficiently to your dog that the action he was doing at that exact moment was desirable. By building up this good association he should start to ignore the other possible responses and begin to offer the correct behaviour every time. For example, when teaching your dog not to

*Treat in the right hand, clicker in the left – when he performs a '**Sit**' on command, you are going to learn how to 'click-treat'.*

*Above: This style of training is called **Instant** because it concentrates on rewarding a dog the **instant** that he performs the behaviour that you want. Your timing is critical.*

jump up to greet people it is very likely that he will try to jump up even after the training to '**Sit**' has started. Over time, if he is rewarded every time he sits first, and if he either cannot make the mistake (perhaps by the use of a house-line) or if no reward occurs when he jumps (if the person turns away, completely ignoring him) then eventually he will learn that sitting in this circumstance is the best option. Once a strong association has been built, he should perform this reliably each time he approaches to say hello.

Don't Reward The Wrong Thing
Training may be slow or unsuccessful if you don't get your timing right and reward him while he is doing the right action. Since your dog is trying to build associations (and not using human logic), he will find it very difficult to pick up the training quickly if you reward him after he has finished the action and gone on to something else. If you are not focused and miss the opportunity to reward him **instantly**, then the chances are that he will have moved or be focused on something different. Indeed your mistimed reward could encourage that random movement or activity instead. Try to be aware of your dog and practise responding as soon as he does something you like; he's very bright and will begin to adapt his behaviour to maximise the praise and rewards he is offered.

You have to be patient and consistent throughout your training plan. The speed at which your dog learns some tasks will delight you. Dogs have been shown to have remarkable ability to learn and remember commands with one dog learning to respond to over 1000 different words. While your dog may never be that sort of verbal genius, there is no doubt that many new commands can be successfully taught.

INTRODUCTION

Relish The Challenge

Unlike your car, computer or mobile phone, your dog cannot be taken in for a quick service when things go wrong, or be exchanged for a more advanced model when the first doesn't function perfectly. Relinquishing a dog to a rescue shelter is a solution that is commonly adopted when

Above: It is a sad fact that many dogs are given up to rescue by owners who are unable to cope with them. Responsible owners must realise that a dog requires real commitment.

things get tricky, but pressure is high on these centres and suitable homes are not readily available, especially for dogs with problems. For this reason it is very important to try to consistently encourage your dog to perform desirable behaviours. This book

Right: 'Little and often' can be our watchword. The training programme outlined in this book suggests that you should take moments out of your busy day to perform some short training exercises. The benefits of repetition will soon become obvious.

It is very important to try to consistently encourage your dog to perform desirable behaviours

is not meant to replace the need for training classes or behavioural support where needed. It aims to provide you with some ideas of how to include training in the different areas of your daily routine. Of course, it will require some extra time commitment, especially when you first begin training a new activity, but you will both benefit from regular interaction with your dog and the development of good canine habits.

Below: Problems will inevitably crop up when you own a dog, like scavenging. But effective training gives you a powerful tool to shape canine behaviour.

It is easy to label a dog 'naughty' or a 'problem' but most owners have bad habits too. By understanding a little bit more about your pet, it is hoped that you can avoid some of the common pitfalls and achieve more than you expected. Owning a dog is a real responsibility, but with this responsibility comes a huge amount of enjoyment that makes all the effort worthwhile.

The Good News

Now that the importance of training has been identified, we can focus on how you can best get it done.

So what exactly is involved in dog training? Dog training often conjures up images of standing in a freezing cold field or community centre for hours, or shouting 'Fido Sit, Fido Down' repeatedly. Luckily for both dogs and owners, it should be much more fun than that! Training is not the same as forcing or threatening your dog to comply. A well-trained dog is one that has been taught to want to behave or respond in a way that we like.

So how do you get started? Our lifestyles are busier than ever and many otherwise dedicated dog owners just cannot commit to a regular evening or weekend training class. While a good class will help to guide you and your dog through the necessary lessons

*Left: You can even fit in a quick '**Fetch**' exercise when you are sitting down watching television. **Instant** training seizes the moment and weaves training into the daily routine.*

Despite having a busy routine, this book shows how **you will be able to guide and train your dog as you go about your daily life**. Dog training certainly doesn't have to be, and in fact should not be, a boring chore that you slog away at for hours each day. Adjusting your routine to include regular focus on your pet will help you to achieve better behaviour and training responses. Of course, it would be misleading to suggest you that you do not have to spend much time with your dog. Your dog is a social species that has evolved to put great focus upon his interactions with humans. He deserves to enjoy time with his pack (that's you and your family) and this is something that you will have to make sure he will experience.

With increased input of time and training from you, your dog's behaviour is likely to improve, meaning that he can be involved in more and more activities with you and your family. The result? A happy dog and a happy owner. So, let's get started today!

Right: Training a dog is a journey that you make together. If you get it right, it's one of the most rewarding experiences that you can share.

*Above: It is generally beneficial to take a dog to an organised training class but not everyone can fit classes into a busy schedule. **Instant** training puts the class in your own home.*

and will help to motivate you week by week, not being able to attend regularly should not mean that you don't train your dog at all.

CHAPTER 1

UNDERSTANDING YOUR DOG

To maximise your ability to train your dog, it is critical that you know how to communicate with him. It's possible to learn to recognise signals from your dog which will allow you to interpret how he is feeling at any given time. Your dog has evolved alongside humans for so long that he has actually adapted to respond to some of our gestures and even has the ability to read our facial expressions.

Dogs are obligatory pack animals. This means that they are highly adapted to live in groups and have developed a series of ways of trying to calm or appease other pack members. The advantage of this is that they can avoid tensions escalating into aggression and pos-

It's important for all owners to be able to 'read' their dog's behaviour. After all, misinterpretation could potentially have serious consequences. Missing the signs that your dog is stressed could mean that you continue to do something that he finds threatening or accidentally encourage a behaviour that you don't like. Both can lead to more problematic behaviour. It is also very important to be aware of the mistake of being anthropomorphic (assigning human attributes) when interpreting your dog's behavioural signs as there are significant differences.

New car drivers are expected to understand the basic workings of their vehicle before they begin driving. Imagine if we started our cars without knowing the function of the ped-

Above: Living peacefully with other pack members relies on a complex array of signals designed to appease and calm one another. These allow large groups of dogs to live together in relative harmony.

sible injury. If we can recognise these calming mechanisms, it is possible to respond appropriately and avoid confrontations. Some of these signals include yawning and fast flicks of the tongue across the lips; signs you may instantly dismiss if you don't know what to look for.

Above: Little flicks of the tongue over the muzzle when another dog approaches can be a pacifying gesture to show that this dog has no aggressive intent and wants to avoid any direct confrontation.

Below: When dogs meet, they size one another up by reading signals expressed by posture, scent and demeanour.

Specific body language signals and actions can be considered as separate letters or sounds in the alphabet. You need to be able to recognise them but by themselves they probably don't tell you the whole story. As you become familiar with each signal, you will find it easier to put the signs together and interpret your dog's intention correctly.

The breed of dog will have an impact on how easily it can be read. We have morphed the canine body into so many shapes and sizes through selective breeding that we have altered their natural ability to express them-

als or gearstick! It is highly advantageous if dog owners also acquire some knowledge of their pets before they bring them home. While this book cannot teach you the intricacies of canine communications and doesn't expect you to become a canine specialist, there are some signs that will help you on a daily basis.

Reading Your Dog

When you 'read' your dog you are trying to interpret what he is asking for; whether this is for more contact or for you to move away.

We have created a huge diversity of canine body forms through selective breeding. Some of these characteristics can make it harder to read a dog's body language.

It's important for all owners to be able to 'read' their dog's behaviour

Above: Communicating with a dog during training is a two-way street – he must be able to 'read' you, just as you must endeavour to 'read' him.

selves. This includes those with curly tails, floppy ears, wrinkled faces, heavy jowls, long or heavy coats, shortened muzzles, docked or absent tails and those black dogs whose eyes and facial expressions are easily missed. Reading these dogs is a little like reading a very fancy type-font; it takes a little time and focus but once you recognise the common pattern, it becomes easier. As the owner you are the best person to notice subtle changes in your dog's demeanour.

UNDERSTANDING YOUR DOG

Fearful   Natural variations in ear position   Alert and confident

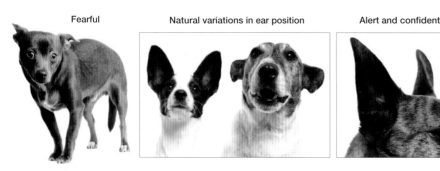

Ears

Your dog's breed impacts on the way his ears look. It is normal for the ears to move as your dog focuses on you during training. The direction of his ears will also change when he is distracted. Emotions are also expressed by ear position. If his ears are flattened backwards on his head, then this indicates extreme submission or fear. Upright, forward-facing ears indicate a more confident response which is what you look for in training. Your dog may show ear positions at any stage between the forward-facing and flattened positions depending upon his exact emotions.

Friendly grin

Aggressive

Muzzle and Teeth

There are many misunderstandings about what it means to see your dog's teeth. Many people, including children, assume their dog is smiling at them. Others panic at the first sign of teeth and assume their dog has an extreme dominance problem. It's important to get this right as a mistake may be disastrous. Seeing bared teeth can be a real cause for concern but this may not be an overtly aggressive response. If your dog has a wide gaping mouth and is exposing all his teeth, then it is most likely that he is expressing fear or appeasement. You will probably see his ears drawn back, low body posture and possibly some lip-smacking at the

Whites exposed, fearful **Hard stare**

Eyes

Eye shape will change depending upon the amount of facial tension but this may be difficult to observe in overly hairy dogs. Extremely wide eyes exposing the whites of the eyeball are associated with fear. Partially closed, squinty or blinking eyes are often seen when a dog is trying to appease or is acknowledging another's control over a resource. A hard stare could be a challenging signal but be careful in your interpretation since a frightened dog will also watch you closely as any of us would watch something that's potentially dangerous. In training, your dog's eyes should look alert and responsive.

Yawning

Although this may be sometimes associated with tiredness, this action is most often exhibited when a dog is trying to appease and pacify another individual or when he's feeling a little stressed or conflicted. Again it implies that your dog may not be in the right frame of mind for training.

Tongue

Prior to biting, a dog will draw his tongue back into his mouth safely away from his teeth. A lolling tongue therefore indicates that he is not intending to bite at that moment.

same time. Some dogs show an appeasing grin whenever they greet their family or new people. If, however, your dog has curled his lips upwards, wrinkling his muzzle to expose his large canine teeth at the front, then this is a clear signal of overt aggression. Either way, take care as your dog could be under a great deal of stress and could react aggressively towards you.

Lip-smacking

This is when the dog quickly flicks the tongue forwards and upwards. This indicates a pacifying gesture but if the threat continues it may precede more direct warnings or extreme avoidance responses. This is a sign of stress; the dog needs to relax before any training.

Left: A dog may smack his lips and flick his tongue rapidly over his nose and muzzle as a pacifying gesture signifying that no threat is intended. It is thought to derive from the young pup's behaviour used to solicit food from the mother.

UNDERSTANDING YOUR DOG

The low body carriage and tucked-under tail reveal anxiety.

We might interpret this posture and facial expression as revealing guilt, but really the dog is apprehensive because he can 'read' your displeasure.

Standing Tall This is usually a sign of confidence. However, some dogs that feel threatened will stand tall to try to appear larger, and therefore be more likely to scare the other dog or person away. Trainers need to look at other physical signals to interpret the standing tall posture more clearly.

Exposing the belly is a gesture of extreme appeasement.

A tight muzzle and flattened ears also express fear.

Cowering Anxious and fearful dogs hold themselves low to the ground and make themselves as small as possible. They may expose their stomachs in a sign of appeasement and non-threat. These dogs should be approached carefully; ideally giving them time and space to recover some confidence to approach you instead. Dogs express appeasement gestures when their owner is angry. This occurs whether or not they have genuinely done something to trigger the anger. The appeasement is a response to the owner's reaction so don't ever take this as proof of 'guilt'.

Barking Although your dog's bark may draw your attention more than other forms of expression, vocalisation is one of the least significant methods of canine communication. Your dog's bark will have different meanings depending upon the circumstance. Try to observe his body language at the same time to give you a better interpretation of what he is trying to say.

Positioning If your dog chooses to move away from you, another person, or a dog, then this is an excellent signal to say he needs space. This may be subtle and may only involve him turning his head away from you, or he may physically separate himself completely. It's not a good time to start training.

Hackles

Raised hackles occur when the hair along your dog's back becomes erect. People often assume this signals aggression when usually it means the dog is feeling uncomfortable and is trying to make himself appear bigger to make the thing that's scaring him go away. This may escalate into more overt aggression if the scary individual continues to threaten. Take care if your dog raises his hackles when you are out, perhaps heel-training. It's a sign of unease.

The raised hackles and snarl may indicate fear rather than outright aggressive intent.

Your dog can only communicate using his natural range of instinctive canine signals. As owners and trainers we must try to correctly interpret and respond to our dog's messages.

Play-Bow

When your dog is trying to instigate play, he may bend his elbows, lowering the front half of his body. This may be done while standing still or while bouncing around enthusiastically. Trainers will recognise the play-bow as an invitation to have fun.

Tails

Tail wagging often occurs when your dog is greeting another dog or person and is often assumed to indicate a happy, friendly character. However, in truth tail wagging can signal different intentions. Try to observe the tail position while it's wagging. A loose wag in an approximately horizontal position usually indicates a friendly greeting. A tail wagged lower down may be an attempt to appease the approaching human or dog, while a stiff, upright wag indicates that the dog is feeling very confident and assertive.

If your dog has a docked tail then you will have to watch closely for movement. You may observe the entire rear end moving. Be aware that some breeds, in particular some of the terriers, naturally hold their tails upright and this may be misinterpreted by humans and dogs alike.

UNDERSTANDING YOUR DOG

Saying What You Mean

The way in which you behave around your dog will also have a great impact on his behaviour. Of course, our instinctive behaviours are often at odds with the way our dogs communicate and we have to be very careful to avoid problems. Unfortunately, our mistakes are common reasons why a dog may bite, especially with children who do not know how to interact appropriately. Unfortunately the dog usually gets the blame for the failure in communication.

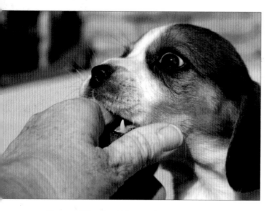

Above: We should not always blame a dog who bites – our own actions around the dog can give rise to tension that eventually boils over.

How Do We Differ?

Clever Dogs Dogs have evolved alongside humans for so long that they have actually adapted to be able to respond to our facial expressions and even some gestures. This fantastic ability is unique to the domestic dog. Dogs that have been brought up with

Above: Instinctively a dog would interpret this action of leaning over him as a sign of threat.

lots of human contact can learn to accept a lot of our more unusual ways and mixed messages. They may become familiar with our habit of leaning over to greet them and with our insistence on making direct eye contact. However, when they are ill or already under stress their tolerance levels will be lower and this should always be remembered.

Hugging Human beings like to show affection and love by hugging our families and friends and we carry our young against our bodies or in our arms. This does not occur naturally between canines and so it can cause a great deal of difficulty with dogs that have not been taught to like being lifted or hugged by people. Most dogs look uncomfortable while being squeezed.

Snuggling and Kissing We like to get our faces up close to people we are fond of, but this may be interpreted as a threatening gesture by your dog. Dogs are usually very careful about the way they approach and look at one another. They rarely go head-to-head, eyeball to eyeball unless they are giving direct challenges. Small children tend to approach quickly, place their faces up close and throw their arms around their pet. Unfortunately, these same small children are unlikely to recognise their dog's attempts to ask

Below: We love to lift small dogs up in our arms and hug them, but remember that this is not natural for them. Initially it can create apprehension.

Above: Take care when children are around dogs; they often want to get right up close and do not sense the dog's rising stress levels.

them to give them space; namely trying to turn their head away, licking their lips or yawning. When these passive signals don't work, the dog is left with little option but to try more direct approaches to achieve the space they require. This is when the dog growls or even snaps. Although this is often reported as an 'out of the blue' reaction, the dog has probably tried very hard to get his message across but has not been understood.

Above: A dog's action of licking around a person's lips derives from the behaviour that young puppies use to solicit food from adults.

Physical Contact, Gesturing and Leaning Over Dogs communicate through a series of subtle behavioural changes – the smallest movement can signal a great deal. Of course humans also have complex behavioural interactions but much of this is done subconsciously and as a result of subtle cues that we detect from the people around us and interpret intuitively without subjecting them to conscious analysis. Since we rely on a different range of signals, we may not be as aware of the consequences of our actions around our dogs. When we lean over them, throw an arm around them, or even try to incite physical interaction, such as wrestling or tickling games, our dogs may not appreciate our intentions. It may be meant in jest or as a sign of affection but these actions may seem threatening to our dogs or may incite unexpected responses.

Smiling In most species the showing of the teeth is a portrayal of the animal's greatest weaponry, and therefore a threat. In contrast, great big wide smiles are our signal of happiness. It's important to remember not to interpret your dog's action in human terms.

Below: 'Leave it alone!' There is no mistaking what the snarl and hard stare are meant to imply, and the young puppy has got the message.

Below: Humans are unusual in using an expression that shows our teeth to signal pleasure and enjoyment. To most other animals, the display of teeth indicates a threat.

UNDERSTANDING YOUR DOG

Using Body Language During Training

Since dogs pay so much attention to physical gestures it is sensible to incorporate these into our 'Instant Training' regime. Specific gestures can be associated with particular commands while other movements may be used to indicate an invitation or a 'not now' signal.

When you are teaching your basic commands, it is helpful to introduce a specific hand signal that is associated with that particular action. This can be recognised by your dog (if you've practised enough) and can speed up the process. You can

The hand gesture backs up the 'Wait' command.

Above: As trainers, we should use our body language to reinforce the training message.

then use hand signal, a verbal cue or a combination of both to elicit an **instant** response from your dog.

If your dog is trying to gain your attention or you sense that he's about to jump up, it can be helpful to physically turn away from him. Dogs use this type of movement as an indication that they do not wish to interact and we can use it to similar effect. If your dog is calmly approaching or nudging at you, then a subtle head turn will probably express your wishes clearly. If, on the other hand, your dog is excitable and persistent, you may need to turn your whole body away and fold your arms.

If your dog is particularly wary, then you will need to make yourself small by crouching down, turning your head away so that you avoid direct eye contact. Hold out a hand

It is helpful to introduce a specific hand signal that is associated with that particular action

Eloquent body language: 'Get down and stop pestering me.'

with some treats for your dog to approach and sniff. Nervous dogs will need different gestures to confident ones when you teach your recall command. Turning away from your dog will make you easier to approach. On the other hand, you can use open-arm gestures and excitable movements to encourage a confident dog to become excited and rush up to you.

Left: Wide-open arms and a lowered body position back up the message: 'Come to me!'

This dog is confident and eager to approach.

Crouch down low and avert your eyes when approaching a fearful dog.

The treats are offered in an open hand.

The turn of the body is a pacifying gesture.

Be aware:
- Your voice and facial expressions are important; try to appear relaxed and friendly.
- Pulling the lead taut removes any option your dog has of avoiding a stressful situation and so he's likely to feel more anxious.
- Keeping moving will prevent stand-off confrontations from occurring.
- Grabbing the collar to pull your dog away could trigger an aggressive response.
- Walk on and call your dog to you, or use his lead to gently guide him away if necessary; moving closer might increase tensions or give your dog the back-up he needs to react.

Your cues will also influence your dog during social encounters. Your dog is so attuned to tension within his social group that if you are concerned as you approach another dog or a person, then this is likely to result in him feeling tense too.

Left: When unfamiliar dogs meet and they are both on the lead, tension can develop. The physical restraint prevents the dogs from engaging freely in the exploratory greeting behaviour that they would normally use to size one another up, while any tension that you may be feeling can also be communicated down the lead.

GET READY FOR INSTANT TRAINING

Being prepared is central to achieving success with your training. This means having the right tools for the job. If you are going to train your dog successfully as you go about your daily routine, then you will need to get organised.

Understanding The Concepts

Being a good trainer and having a dog that's reliably under control does not mean that you must be bossy, aggressive or physically menacing.

Right: Training is not about dominating a dog; it's about building a relationship of mutual trust.

Left: The human family is, in some ways, a pack structure which embodies certain rules of behaviour. A dog does not find it wholly unfamiliar.

Additionally, good behaviour is not dependent upon you being dominant or your dog being submissive. Some dogs can be coerced into behaving in a specific manner, but when they are frightened and stressed most dogs will begin to respond by exhibiting extreme appeasement, fear or defensive aggression. No owner wants to be in this situation.

Through the process of domestication, your dog's natural social order has changed. Luckily, a natural dog pack is very similar to the human family structure in which dogs now find themselves. That is why we work so well together. If you focus on encouraging the right behaviours, building trust between your dog and yourself, and setting good patterns of behaviour, you will achieve great results.

Instant Rewards

Studies have shown that well-timed rewards will accelerate the training process. Without encouragement your dog will not be able to identify the behaviours you like most and will be less likely to repeat them. A reward is **anything** that your

Small morsels of food are the backbone of our training regime. They are used to treat a dog who has responded as we wish, and so they reinforce the desired behaviour.

Your dog will also find pats and strokes pleasurable, so your touch and words of praise can also be used as a training reward.

Right: Once you have trained a behaviour successfully, fade out the treat reward, but offer it randomly every now and then to keep your dog focused.

dog finds pleasurable. We most commonly use food rewards because our bodies need food to survive and eating is a pleasurable experience in itself. Treats are classed as a **primary reinforcer**. This means that by themselves they are enough to evoke a positive response. Since all healthy dogs eat, it is normally possible to use food to encourage repetition of certain behaviours.

Some owners only wish to use their dog's kibble as rewards. While this may work for some training tasks, many dogs will find other activities more interesting than focusing on the biscuits and will therefore be less motivated to train. This is particularly likely if your dog is over-fed at meal times or does not burn off excess energy each day. You should be prepared to offer a reward that your dog adores for more challenging training tasks.

Other than when you are luring your dog into position at the start of a new training task, it should not be necessary to always have treats in your hand when you train. They can remain in your pouch or tub ready to offer the **instant** when your dog gets it right. Focus on getting your timing right,

> Focus on getting your timing right, practise being quick with your rewards...

practise being quick with your rewards and develop good hand signals and verbal associations.

Once the training aim has been achieved and your dog is performing the action reliably, you can begin to fade out the offer of treats for that particular task. However, you should only do this when your dog is offering the correct response every time or you may find his response gradually deteriorates. Do not suddenly stop offering rewards altogether. Keep your dog guessing at what may be coming by offering him treats randomly for correct responses to known tasks. Continue to offer praise to ensure the desirable behaviour remains his first choice.

Below: The choice of food treat is huge these days. Make sure that you select something that your dog loves so that he'll be motivated to seek the reward.

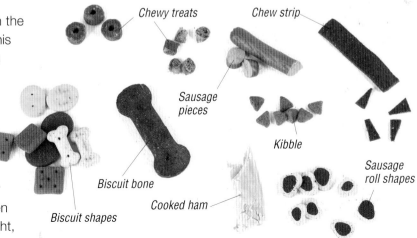

Chewy treats

Chew strip

Sausage pieces

Kibble

Sausage roll shapes

Biscuit bone

Cooked ham

Biscuit shapes

GET READY FOR INSTANT TRAINING

Remind yourself that dogs will repeat behaviours that bring a rewarding experience. This means that good training should focus on encouraging

Dogs will repeat behaviours that bring a rewarding experience

desirable behaviour and preventing the dog from discovering how much fun 'naughty' behaviour can be.

If you get your timing of rewards right, then you can have speedy and efficient training success. Don't waste a training opportunity; be ready to praise all good behaviour and **instantly** offer rewards for actions you specifically want to reinforce. Aim to offer a reward within a couple of seconds of the desirable action. Dogs don't respond well to a delayed reward, so giving a biscuit for good behaviour on a walk when you get home will not have the desired effect. Likewise, observing a good response and then having to go through to another room to find some treats in a cupboard will also be ineffective. By the time you

give your dog the treat, his focus will be on something else, probably you getting a treat from the cupboard, and he will have no idea that it relates to his earlier response.

What if..?

Your dog has a sensitive digestion or is dieting? In these cases you should take care to select food types that your dog can tolerate or low-fat options. It may be possible to use his kibble under these circumstances. If your dog is on a diet, he may be very keen to earn any extra pieces of biscuit. There are many types of treats that you can buy including cooked meats. Try very small squares of turkey or baked fish to see whether he can tolerate these options.

Above: Use a portion of your dog's daily ration of kibble if you are concerned about the effect of too many treats on his waistline.

Your dog isn't fussed by treats? All dogs eat and so it is usually possible to find something that he is motivated to work for. However, it is possible to use toys and playtime if

Above: Some dogs enjoy training using toys as their reward, but you have to retrieve the toy before the next training exercise can begin.

that's what your dog adores. This is trickier since once he has the toy, you have to retrieve it before you can repeat the training task.

Clicker Training

One way to 'mark' desirable behaviour is to try the clicker training technique. The clicker can be the key to **instant** training as it allows you to reinforce desirable behaviour as soon as it happens, whenever it happens, by making an audible signal.

A clicker is a small device that gives out a 'click' sound when an internal metal tongue is depressed by your finger. This 'click' sound is clear and consistent and can therefore be instantly paired up with food which allows you to use the clicker to reinforce activities that you would like to encourage your dog to perform. The 'click' becomes what we term as a **secondary reinforcer** meaning that it is associated with the primary reward, the treat. Clicker training benefits owners and dogs since it encourages you to look for good behaviour to 'click' rather than only focusing on your dog's mistakes. It is far more encouraging for both you and your dog to look at the positive actions rather than only responding to things you dislike.

To pair up the 'click' sound and

Right: A clicker makes a consistent click noise whenever its mechanism is activated. It can be used to precisely 'mark' a good behaviour.

treats is simple and your training success will be faster if your dog already understands that the click means 'Yes!'

Pour out your dog's kibble into a bowl or into a training pouch. If he is not keen on the kibble or eats wet food, you can use small dog treats or pieces of meat. Offer your dog a piece of food and 'click' as he takes it. Repeat this several times so that he can learn that the 'click' is paired with the arrival of something edible. If you do this enough times, your dog will begin to anticipate a treat whenever he hears the 'click'. This will be extremely valuable later on when you're training.

The dog knows that a 'click' means a treat.

Charging A Clicker
This preparatory exercise makes your dog associate the sound of a click with the arrival of a treat as a reward.

*Click the clicker that you are holding and **instantly** give your dog a treat. Repeat the 'click-treat' sequence several times so the dog learns that a 'click' equals a treat.*

You can also 'click' and then throw the treat onto the floor for your dog to enjoy. When he looks back at you, repeat the process.

GET READY FOR INSTANT TRAINING

Once your dog has made the association, his reaction to the sound of the 'click' will be automatic. He will learn to repeat behaviours that result in a 'click' and so you can use the clicker to reinforce any activity or emotional response thereafter. You may prefer to lure your dog to perform a specific activity at first or you may want to seize the moment when your dog does something unexpected but desirable. Either way, always encourage actions you like and you will see them begin to occur more often.

Each 'click' should be followed **instantly** by a reward or your dog will begin to respond less and less to the sound. Be prepared to 'click' often at first and then, once the behaviour has started to fall into place, begin to expect slightly more from your dog before he earns the '**click-treat**'.

As you become more familiar with your clicker and have a clear idea in your mind about what it is that you wish your dog to do, you will become more precise in your timing. The closer to the desired action that the 'click' occurs, the more likely it is that your dog will recognise the specific action that brings a reward.

'Click' only when your dog is behaving well or you will encourage the wrong response. Make sure that other family members also understand this and that children do not play with the

Incorrect
This example shows a mistimed 'click' as the puppy is lagging behind the handler. The reward signal came too early. In heelwork, you are waiting for the moment when your dog is walking alongside you. Only then should you 'click' and reward.

Correct
We can see here a puppy walking nicely alongside the handler. The 'click' occurs at the correct time and is immediately followed with an edible treat reward. It helps that the dog is still in the correct place when the treat is offered.

A target stick extends your reach.

This dog is learning that a 'click' and treat come when he touches the red ball.

Both above: A target stick is a valuable training aid. You can teach a dog to target the end of the stick held in various positions with his nose by using the 'click-treat' technique.

Right: This clicker is nicely shaped to fit comfortably in the hand and features a large press button that is activated by the thumb.

clicker. When not in use, leave the clicker where you can easily find it, but make sure that your dog cannot root it out and chew it, as this could be hazardous if bits were swallowed.

Target Stick This usually takes the form of an extendable wand or stick which acts as an extension of your arm to aid training. You first spend time targeting your dog to touch the end of the stick, either with his nose, paw or other body part. The easiest way to start this is to rub a treat on the end of the stick and hold it out for your dog to sniff. As he does so, 'click' and treat. Repeat this until he is readily touching the stick when you hold it out, no matter whether this is to the left, right, low down or high up. Now you can use the target stick to encourage a range of movements and tricks.

What You Will Need For Training

A Clicker You will need to have your clicker to hand so that you can use it quickly and easily. After all, there's no point in having an instant signal of reward if it take a few minutes to find it! Many clickers come with a lanyard or belt clip and some have a finger band

If you practise… you will see positive results

that means you can slip them over your finger like a ring. All these aspects make it easier for you to respond in time to encourage good behaviour. Keep one in your treat pouch and

some others in different places so you always have one to hand.

What if...?
Your dog is worried by noises?
When you begin training, you should take care not to startle your dog before he has had a chance to learn that the 'click' signals something enjoyable. When you start, muffle the sound by holding the clicker up your sleeve or inside your pocket. Offer very tasty treats to build a positive association quickly.

You already use praise and rewards? Although clicker training can benefit many training programmes, you certainly do not need to use one for all training and interaction with your dog. However, verbal praise is less effective because your dog hears you talking a lot without his actions being reinforced with a treat. If you practise using a specific word and tone of voice to indicate that your dog's done something right, you will see positive results. You may want to use the clicker to reinforce an activity that is particularly tricky but you should continue to offer praise too.

GET READY FOR INSTANT TRAINING

Treat Tubs You should be prepared to pay your dog for good behaviour, especially when the new response is in its early stages and has not yet become established. By making sure that your dog experiences something pleasurable each time he tries out a new response, you will see results quickly.

For Instant Training to be effective, you need to reward **instantly** too. Prepare by setting treat pots in various positions around the home so that no matter where you are, you can reinforce good behaviour. Food containers that lock

Edible rewards will speed up the learning process

Above: You may have to be prepared to use whatever food your dog is willing to work for.

What if..?

Your dog doesn't like treats? Of course some dogs are less motivated by food than others. However, the very fact that your dog is alive tells us that he must eat. Try to use some of your dog's daily food allowance for training treats to increase his motivation to earn them. If he is offered a lot of rich food and snacks at other times, then he will be less inclined to work for occasional treats so try to keep all tasty foods just

Below: A belt-mounted treat pouch is a very handy item when you are training 'on the go'. The treats are right at your fingertips.

Above: Plastic treat tubs with airtight lids stop the smell of the food permeating the room.

Above: These chunks can be neatly stashed in a treat pouch for timely use during training.

shut are useful for this as they also reduce the scent of food that may otherwise attract your dog. It is possible to use treat pouches too. These are very useful on walks but you may not always wish to wear a pouch while you are at home. Also your dog may learn that rewards only come when you are

wearing it and so he is likely to reduce his good responses when he cannot see the pouch around your waist. Treat tubs should be positioned out of your dog's reach and should be easy to open just when you need them. Also, remember to top them up regularly.

for training. If your dog is fussy, try to find different types of treat or use pieces of cooked meat. There is usually something for every dog. Some dogs won't eat because they are stressed or afraid. In that case you will have to try to address this anxiety problem first.

Below: Some dogs love chase and retrieve games and can even catch Frisbees in mid-air.

Below: Dogs' toys can take quite a beating. Ideally, choose strong and durable ones.

Toys There has never been so many options of toys for dogs to play with as there are available today. There's a range of safe playthings to suit most styles of game play. Your dog should have access to toys that suit his size and character. If he is a prolific chewer, then select large, tough toys. If he adores chasing things, then balls and Frisbee-type toys will interest him. Different types of toys will be needed for different occasions. You should be ready to provide him with toys to encourage independent play when you are busy or when you leave him alone, and other types of toy for interactive play. Toys that you take on walks to throw may not be as durable as the ones he gets to spend time chewing on at home.

Below: Each toy has a purpose and can help you to train and encourage good behaviours throughout the day.

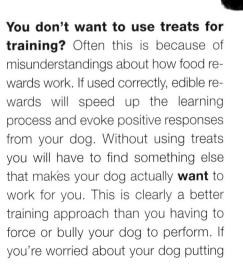

You don't want to use treats for training? Often this is because of misunderstandings about how food rewards work. If used correctly, edible rewards will speed up the learning process and evoke positive responses from your dog. Without using treats you will have to find something else that makes your dog actually **want** to work for you. This is clearly a better training approach than you having to force or bully your dog to perform. If you're worried about your dog putting on weight, then ensure that the overall amount of food he eats in the day is consistent. This means that if he's earned lots of rewards in the course of the day, then you should reduce his meal size correspondingly.

Don't worry that you will be forced to use treats forever once you have started. Once your dog has learned to respond to the new command, you can gradually reduce the number you offer until you only use the occasional treat on a random basis.

CHAPTER 2

GET READY FOR INSTANT TRAINING

Leads and Lines Using a lead or an indoor houseline will provide you with a great deal of control without the need to chase or confront your dog at any time. Having control over your dog at a distance allows you all to remain calm and patient while your dog learns how to respond. You may wish to have a training line for work within the home. These are often much lighter and longer than a regular lead and your dog can trail it behind him at times when you are present to supervise. Lines should

lines are best attached to a buckle collar or a harness. If your dog needs training in the garden, then get into the habit of leaving the line at the door so it's available every time you need it. Consistency is the key to success!

What if...?
Your dog doesn't wear a collar?
While training is going on, you should fit your dog with a collar or even a harness. You can take these off at night or when training is not occurring. Legally all dogs, other than those out working, should wear a collar and identification tag even if they are micro-chipped or tattooed with details of their identity and owner.

Below: A long line for outdoor use tends to be sturdier and longer than a houseline. It allows you to practise recall training while your dog is some way away from you, safe in the knowledge that he cannot stray too far.

Call the puppy back to you.

And praise him for coming.

Above: A houseline provides you with the means of keeping control over a dog while you are indoors. You can even use it to start some basic recall training with a young puppy in the safety of the home.

clip to your dog's buckle collar but never to a check-chain. Slip-leads are not suitable for this purpose as they can pull tight if caught up.

Longer lines are available and can help you train your dog to recall reliably. While you are training, take one on every walk although you should use a short lead when your dog is walking next to you by the side of roads. Long

Take care that the trailing line does not get snagged.

The treat is the reward for coming when called.

Above: Body harnesses are available in sizes to fit all types of dogs and puppies. They are especially useful with dogs that pull on the lead.

Your dog likes chewing? Some dogs will chew through a houseline when left to their own devices. The line is a training tool and so you should be present while he is wearing it. Try to ensure your dog has something to keep him distracted so his focus does not linger on the line. Some owners find that a tough plastic washing line with a metal core provides enough strength while also slipping around the edges of furniture easily. It is cheap and easy to cut off a new length if necessary. Others find success by spraying some bitter-tasting deterrent spray onto the line before use. Either way, you

Right: If your dog gets into the habit of chewing on his lead or houseline, try spraying it with a bitter deterrent spray. He mustn't view the lead as another toy.

should always take care that your dog is safe during all training exercises. A houseline is a temporary measure. Until your dog is used to it, he may try to chew it.

What Do You Expect?

I hope that all owners will aim high with respect to their dog's behaviour and training but in the same breath, it is important to be realistic. Just as people vary in their ability to master a particular skill, dogs also vary. Some will be naturally inclined to behave in a certain way, others will require varying degrees of training, and some will have skills in another area entirely. It is up to each owner to make sure that they attempt to get the very

Above: A dog that is trained to walk calmly to heel is a pleasure to have as a companion.

best from their dog, and to ensure that he is safe both in the home and when out in public places.

All breeds need to be trained to behave well. Even if your dog is going to be a lap dog, you will still want him to be friendly and allow you to brush and groom him, examine him for injuries, walk without pulling and be able to introduce him to your friends, strangers, their kids and other dogs. The reality of being a pet dog is that they have to be able to adapt successfully to a vast range of situations from day to day which really is a challenge. If you've purchased a working breed, then don't assume he will be clever enough to train himself either; clever breeds can get into more mischief than you may ever imagine!

GET READY FOR INSTANT TRAINING

Who's The Trainer? The best achievements come from regular, consistent training and encouragement of good behaviour. It is usual for one member of the household to take on most

Right: Often one family member takes the lead role in training.

Above: Children naturally like to spoil a puppy but this can undermine your training regime.

responsibility for the dog's care and training. This may work in some cases, but can lead to difficulties when other members need to care for the dog or try to instil certain rules during the course of a normal day. Problems are particularly evident when one member actively spoils the dog while the other attempts to regain control in a punitive manner. Problems also occur when an adult physically reprimands the dog or shouts since this is a bad example that the children may try to copy.

Your dog may be clever but he's not a mind reader

Instant Training Tips

1 Create a family rota for your dog's basic care routine so that everyone appreciates all aspects and so your dog isn't focused on just one person.

2 Sit down together today and discuss what house-rules you would like to establish. Once these have been agreed on, stick to them. Changing rules from day to day will only confuse your dog and slow down your progress. **Instant** training can only be effective if you know what you're aiming for.

3 All agree on command words and stick with them. Humans have complex language skills but swapping one word for another is a habit that confuses your dog.

4 Make sure you say clearly what you mean when you're training. Your dog may be clever but he's not a mind reader and won't automatically know what you want him to do.

Below: Make it a house-rule that all members of the family stick to the same words when training the dog. If different people say different things, he'll get confused.

Dog Type Not all dogs are destined to be quiet lap dogs or agility champions. Hopefully, you will have researched your dog's breed type before buying him. If not, it is worth doing so now so that you can fully appreciate his potential talents

Make sure you speak clearly when giving a verbal command.

Above: Different breeds of dog have different abilities and temperaments. Try to research your dog's character to understand him better.

and possible areas where he may struggle. This helps you to manage and train him more effectively since you will find it easier to motivate him and select activities suitable to his stamina and body shape.

Dog Age All dogs can learn and adapt their behaviour to some extent.

Very young puppies are just learning about the world and so change their behaviour readily in response to encouragement and tasty rewards. It is never too early to begin training your puppy. In fact, encouraging desirable behaviour before bad habits creep in is highly rec-

Left: Try to get the family involved in training a new puppy to establish good habits early.

ommended. Of course, while you are training your puppy he will make mistakes, so be prepared for this. Don't get frustrated; this is a normal part of the learning process and it's

Above: Young puppies will have a limited attention span, and will need toilet breaks.

likely that you are also making handling mistakes as you get to know your puppy too.

Your puppy will have a short attention span and will become tired of focusing on the same command for too long. Therefore stick to training sessions of about three minutes in length and then have a break with a game, allowing your puppy to rest, drink or eat, or take a toilet break. While he is teething you should expect him to be

less focused, more irritable or excitable and less inclined to take crunchy treats.

If you own an **older dog**, your training may be in an attempt to combat undesirable habits that have already become established. Be patient as change will probably not be immediate. Remember that the bad habit probably took time to develop too. If your dog is elderly then your training techniques will have to take into consideration changes in his eyesight, hearing, physical ability and even his taste. This may involve larger hand signals, louder, clearer verbal cues, highly scented treats and easier manoeuvres.

Below: You will need patience when training an elderly dog whose senses are on the wane.

CHAPTER 3
PUPPY TRAINING – SOCIALISING

Many owners are caught out by the fact that time is short when it comes to socialisation and habituation opportunities for a young puppy. This is the time when your puppy is learning fast about the world around him and is able to take in and respond to new information and experiences. It comes as a surprise to owners to learn that research has shown that the ideal time for your puppy to have these experiences is before 12 weeks of age. Having lots of enjoyable early experiences allows the puppy to cope with novelty and occasional unpleasant encounters much more robustly than those without this experience.

The ideal time for your puppy to have these experiences is before 12 weeks of age

Below: The process whereby puppies get used to unfamiliar objects is called habituation. Owners should try to introduce a structured programme from an early age.

Owners of a puppy should make socialisation a priority; **which means starting today**. Life with a frightened, anxiety-driven dog is a challenge and many dogs end up being euthanised or re-homed due to related behaviour problems. Socialisation involves teaching your puppy how to interact with people and other animals. Habituation involves your puppy learning to ignore or accept inanimate objects, locations, smells or noises. Both sets of experiences are often grouped together when people discuss puppy socialisation. Both are vital.

Socialisation teaches a puppy how to react to other living creatures.

Above: Puppies are naturally inquisitive about the world around them. They need to learn so much so quickly, but owners must also take care to protect them from dangers, like open water.

The puppy must learn that this is a family pet, not prey!

Create a chart depicting your puppy's experiences. Having a record of how many different people, places, animals, vehicles, sounds, smells and other unfamiliar things that your puppy has seen each day/week will clearly show you in which areas you might need to make more effort. Pre-vaccinated puppies can be safely carried in your arms, taken to your friend's homes (as long as no unvaccinated dogs live there), and they should be exposed to a wide variety of noises.

Above: Even if you have owned many dogs in the past and consider yourself a practised hand, still take your new puppy to training classes. This is your unique opportunity to teach this particular dog good manners.

Above: It pays to make a detailed chart outlining the various sounds and experiences to which your puppy has been introduced, so that you can focus on any deficiencies.

Sign up for your vet clinic's Puppy Party and register for the best puppy class you can find. Even if you have had previous dogs, this is your current puppy's **only** chance to gain critical experience. Many owners who have owned dogs in the past don't take their new dogs to classes since they feel that they already know all the relevant information. This is often a mistake. Each puppy

should be viewed as a blank slate requiring individual focus on training and socialisation, no matter what previous experience the owner has, or how many other dogs are living in the home.

Visitors Ask some friends to come to your home for coffee or drinks. This will allow your puppy to begin to learn about new people coming to the home. Ask your neighbours or work colleagues to drop by too. If they have children, then this is a great opportunity to begin teaching your puppy about how to respond around children. Owning a new puppy is a great excuse to become more sociable yourself!

Encourage other children to visit your puppy; they can even bring their own dogs.

Well supervised meetings with other dogs boost a puppy's confidence.

PUPPY TRAINING – SOCIALISING

Get Driving Your puppy needs to learn to relax while travelling in a vehicle. Often their first experiences of cars are very stressful since they are driven

Don't allow people to rush up to your puppy and scare him

Above: Don't allow other people to pick up your puppy suddenly; it may frighten him.

away from their littermates and mother, and then driven to the vet for vaccinations. Young puppies often experience motion sickness too which adds to their anxiety. Many people safely confine their puppy to a car crate or a car harness. Get your puppy used to this by placing him inside the crate frequently and by fitting the harness while praising and rewarding him. Take him on short journeys; perhaps to post a letter, to visit a nearby friend, or to go the park – he should soon learn to relax while in the car.

You may find that **pheromone therapy for dogs** can help to relax your puppy in the car and speed up the adjustment time. These are sprays that contain synthetic versions of naturally occurring canine pheromones that help to calm anxiety. A quick spray of the product in the car can help to calm down a dog or puppy that is showing signs of anxiety.

Make It Fun Although it is important that your puppy experiences a wide range of events during his early weeks, these events must be enjoyable for him. Make sure that you don't allow

 Above: Puppies need to get used to travelling in cars as car journeys will almost inevitably feature significantly in their future life experiences. However, they must be properly secured inside the car and not allowed to roam free like this.

 Above: The best way to keep a puppy safe inside a car, and to prevent him from possibly distracting the driver, is to put him in a car crate in the back of the vehicle. He can settle in his bed and have access to toys and treats while there.

Above: Ensure that your puppy gets used to you running your hands over his body and examining his eyes, ears, teeth and paws. Use tasty treats to reward compliant behaviour.

people to rush up to your puppy and scare him, to pick him up too quickly or to drop him back down on the floor too hard. If he looks worried (low posture, flattened ears, yawning etc) then you should move him away from the stimulus (the person/dog/object) and allow him to relax before trying again in a slower, less intensive way.

Handling Experience All puppies need to learn to relax when their owners touch them. Each day run your hands all over him praising and rewarding as you go. Your puppy must learn to allow people to touch his paws and check his ears, eyes and teeth even though this is not a normal experience between dogs. Take it slowly and try to take the opportunity throughout the day to handle and reward your puppy.

Older Dog? Many of you will own an older puppy or adult dog. While you will never be able to turn back the sands of time and socialise your dog as effectively as when he was a puppy, it is always advisable to try to set up enjoyable encounters so that your dog

Instead of cuddling him, stay relaxed and wait for his confidence to rise again.

continues to learn about events and so that he adapts his responses. If your dog is already anxious and becomes worried about certain events, then you should endeavour to expose him to those events at a low level (which means either far away from the source of anxiety, or in some way that makes the trigger less scary) while reinforcing confident responses. You should be able to rebuild a desirable reaction. This is the way we desensitise dogs to noises, people, other dogs or traffic. It is very important that you resist the human desire to try to console your dog by hugging or petting him while he is worried. Unfortunately, this will probably only reinforce the anxious behaviour rather than reducing his specific fear. Stay calm and try to encourage only confident, relaxed responses.

Left: It's a very natural reaction to want to reassure a dog that is showing obvious signs of anxiety. However, this can be counter-productive as your actions can reinforce the anxious feelings.

CHAPTER 4
TRAINING THE BASIC COMMANDS

You will first need to spend some time teaching your dog to respond to the basic commands which you can then apply when you need a little more control or a way to encourage better manners. Reinforce these commands many times a day. These commands are suitable for healthy dogs of any age, including puppies.

Before you imagine having to slog through long, laborious training sessions, stop! Think 'Instant'. Training is more manageable and successful if you approach it in short, positive bouts. A few minutes focusing on a particular task is enough per command.
Fit these in while you wait for the kettle to boil, during TV adverts or while dinner is cooking.

Children should observe first while you teach the command. Then, while you closely supervise them, they can follow the same procedure. Take care as children expect fast responses and often give repetitive verbal commands unless you specifically teach them not to.

Get Ready Make sure that you have your treats and your clicker ready for the **instant** when your dog gets it right. Any delay will make the association that you want to instil harder for your dog to make.

Children should follow the example of an adult trainer so that commands are consistent throughout the family.

Sit

All dogs can learn to sit though many are not that reliable and require multiple requests or some pushing and shoving by their owner to get them to obey.

Teach your own dog to **Sit** in a calm, consistent manner and you'll be able to utilise this in many aspects of your daily Instant Training routine.
- Get your dog's attention and encourage him to sniff a titbit in your hand. Resist the temptation to say '**Sit**' at this stage.
- Slowly move the treat up and back over your dog's head so that he raises his

Use a treat to gain your dog's attention when he is standing calmly in front of you.

Draw the treat up and over the dog's head so that his weight moves back as he tries to follow it.

Treat when his bottom touches the ground.

Above: When teaching a small dog or a puppy to Sit, it helps if you kneel down so that you do not loom over the dog from a standing position. Slowly lure his head up and back using very careful hand movements. Small dogs require more precision in this respect.

nose to follow the food. It is natural for your dog to lower his bottom as he does this so he can follow the treat more easily.

• The **instant** your dog's bottom touches the ground, you should give him the treat. If you are using the clicker, then 'click' at this exact moment and then offer the treat.

• Each time your dog goes into position, offer a reward so that he learns that this is a really good position to go into around people.

• With practice your dog will begin to associate the upward hand movement with the sitting position. This will be very useful at a later stage.

• Once your dog can **Sit** easily you can begin to add in the verbal cue '**Sit**'. Say this the **instant** his bottom touches the floor so that he can easily link the word and the action. Once he understands this you will be able to give the verbal command and he will know what you mean.

• Now practise in different locations, on different floor types and with distractions. Each member of the family can practise too so that you all can get a reliable response.

• Once your dog is very responsive to this command, you can begin to offer rewards less frequently. However, always try to acknowledge the correct response with a word of encouragement and praise: '**Good dog!**'

*The hand signal for **Sit**.*

*With practice your dog will learn to respond both to your verbal command to '**Sit**' and the appropriate hand gesture.*

Below: Sometimes when working with a small dog, you may find that he jumps towards the treat. In this case you need to hold it a bit higher so that he doesn't try to snatch it.

Instant Problem Solver

My dog won't pay attention to me: Everyone finds that their dog is distracted from time to time. If your dog ignores the lure, he may have had too many treats already or you may need more enticing treats. Or take a break from training and enjoy a game together. Training sessions are more productive when they are short and focused.

My dog jumps up at the treat: It's easy to inadvertently teach a dog to jump rather than **Sit** by holding the treat just above his head but within reach. Raise the treat a bit higher so the dog stops jumping and sits correctly. Wait for the right position before clicking and instantly treating.

*Right: The dog is now in a nice **Sit** as the treat is out of his immediate range.*

The hand is just that bit higher.

This proves too tempting.

*And the **Sit** is perfect.*

TRAINING THE BASIC COMMANDS

Down

This command can be taught fairly quickly and without stress; which will make it more likely that your dog will **want** to lie down when asked.

- Begin with your dog in the sitting position. Hold a treat close to his nose to act as a lure.
- Slowly lower the treat down towards his front paws so that he has to drop his head to follow it. If you get the speed and the position right, your dog will naturally drop into a **Down** position to make it easier for him to get at the treat.
  - The **instant** his body drops onto the floor, you should praise and release the treat. If you are using the clicker that is the

*Above: A **Down** is a great position to teach if you want your dog to be able to settle in one place for an extended period. It is more comfortable than a **Stand** or a long **Sit**.*

moment to give the 'click' to mark the action, then the treat.
- Practise several times and you will see your dog go down more quickly each time.

- Once your dog is going into the **Down** position, you can add in your verbal cue the **instant** he goes into position each time. Decide among your family which word you will choose for this as there is often confusion between the commands used to ask the dog to lie down and the one meaning 'get off the furniture'! The word you use doesn't matter as long as you all consistently use it to mean the same thing.
- Now your dog has learned the position and the verbal cue, you can begin to straighten up into a more comfortable standing position while you give your hand gesture (which was initially the lure to the floor). Gradually stand up until you are able to gesture to the floor with your

Keep the treat secure in your closed hand.

Move the treat hand steadily and ensure that your dog can't yet get at the reward.

Keep the hand with the treat nice and low just in front of the dog's front paws.

Above: Start with your dog in a Sit position in front of you. Hold a treat to your dog's nose and allow him to sniff it without releasing it.

Above: Keeping the treat close to his nose, slowly move it down towards his front paws so that his nose follows the lure down.

*Above: As your dog follows the treat down to the ground, he will start to rebalance himself by allowing his front legs to fold into a **Down**.*

Right: If your dog is young or liable to lapses in concentration, it pays to use a lead secured under a foot to provide extra control.

Make sure that you allow some play in the lead. If it's too tight, the dog's movements will be restricted.

the praise or 'click' so that he learns to go down and wait. Eventually this will mean that he stays down long enough for you to encourage other actions such as '**Settle**' or even a trick.

• If your dog remains in the **Down** position, then you can encourage this by offering further rewards while he remains patiently in place.

*Below: If you hide the treat under your foot, you can unfold back up into a standing position while your dog maintains the **Down**. Aim to build up duration in a **Down** before the reward is given.*

Instant Problem Solver

My dog doesn't want to go Down: Be patient if your dog takes time to learn this lesson; don't push him down or pull his legs out from under him. That will only prove counter-productive.

It's quick and easy to reveal the treat by lifting your foot.

hand while giving your '**Down**' cue and your dog responds.

• Keep up the 'click-treat' pattern and praise until he is completely reliable and then begin to delay the arrival of

If you are working with a clicker, 'click' now. Otherwise, just release the treat

*Once your dog responds to a hand signal, you'll be able to request a **Down** while you stand up straight. No more bending down required!*

My dog won't stay Down: Some dogs get up as soon as they have been rewarded. Initially prolong the **Down** by swiftly offering another reward before he moves. Hiding a treat under your foot is a good way of quickly revealing a reward once a dog has stayed **Down** for a set time.

Some dogs take longer than others to master the **Down**. If your dog is having trouble, don't resort to pushing or pulling him into position. Be patient and make sure you're practising in a place where your dog is relaxed, on a soft surface, and that you reward every success to build confidence.

*Above: The **instant** that your dog is flat on the floor and remaining still in a **Down**, click and reward by giving him the treat.*

*Above: With practice, you can introduce a verbal '**Down**' command and a hand signal as cues to elicit a **Down** whenever you need it.*

CHAPTER 4
TRAINING THE BASIC COMMANDS

Stand

Teaching your dog to stand is useful since he will have to be examined, groomed, towelled dry and may need to be fitted with a harness. If he knows how to 'Stand' still for you, then this is much easier to achieve.

- Begin with your dog in a sitting position in front of you.
- Hold a treat between your thumb and the flat of your hand. Allow your dog to sniff this but not to take the treat.
- Slowly move your hand horizontally out from your dog's nose, as if drawing

*Above: A **Stand** is useful when a dog has to be examined by a vet, or when being groomed.*

him forwards. He will lean forwards and then **Stand**.

- **Instantly** 'click' and treat or praise and release the treat.

- Repeat this action until he stands up perfectly. This does not take long to achieve.
- You can then add in your verbal cue to '**Stand**' just as he gets up from the **Sit**.
- Once he understands the cue word and recognises your hand gesture (the flat hand held out – *shown right*) he should be willing to approach your hand when he sees it held

This dog is alert and primed for action. He is ideally disposed to respond to training.

Keep the treat secure under your thumb so that he can't yet eat it.

Concentrate on getting your timing spot on.

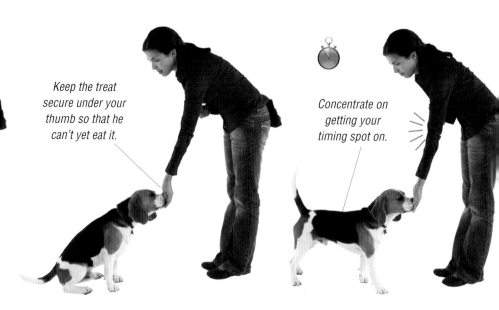

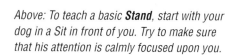

*Above: To teach a basic **Stand**, start with your dog in a Sit in front of you. Try to make sure that his attention is calmly focused upon you.*

Above: Hold a treat just in front of his nose and then slowly move your hand away from him so that he leans forward to follow it.

*Above: As he follows the food, your dog will be lured into the **Stand** position. 'Click-treat' **instantly** and allow him to enjoy the reward.*

Move the treat horizontally out from the dog's nose. If you let your hand drop, he may go into a Down.

*When the dog is consistently moving into a **Stand**, you can straighten up and train while you yourself also stand.*

Above: *If you are training a small dog, get down on the floor so that you are working at his level. Alternatively you can lift the dog onto a secure, non-slip tabletop.*

Above right: *Again use the food lure to encourage your dog to lean forwards. As soon as he stands, click and let him have the treat so that the action is marked and rewarded.*

are slow or move the treats too far away from his nose before letting him have them, he's likely to take several steps forwards.

My dog is small and I'm having trouble with this lesson: You may need to get down on the floor with a small dog or lift them onto a non-slip tabletop. Make sure the treat is moved horizontally away from the dog's nose – too low and he might lie down; too high and he'll jump for it.

*Once your dog is responding consistently, you can begin to add a verbal '**Stand**' command and use a hand signal to maintain the stay.*

out. If you gradually prolong the arrival of the reward, he will learn to stand for greater lengths of time.

Good timing is essential with this task because, if you reward him too late, the chances are that he will have stepped forwards. You want to reinforce the standing position only, so practise clicking and treating at the exact **instant** your dog stands.

Instant Problem Solver

My dog moves forward out of the Stand for the treat: Think about your timing. You must release the reward **instantly** your dog has performed a **Stand**. If you

Above: *As training progresses, build up the time that your dog will **Stand** for you. Treat him intermittently to keep him on his toes.*

It's easier to towel dry a dog who will stand obediently.

TRAINING THE BASIC COMMANDS

Come Back!

All dog owners need to teach their dog to return reliably. This reduces worry for the owner, members of the public and it can also prevent accidents. Some dogs will never be perfect at the recall if they have strong predatory instincts or are known to be livestock chasers. Those dogs need to be trained too, but owners should never take risks by letting them off the lead at inappropriate times and places.

- Your dog needs to be taught that coming when you call is **the most** exciting and rewarding experience. If he thinks this, then you will be able to call him away from most activities and distractions.
- You will need to be patient and con-

Above: A dog that does not reliably return when called is a major cause for concern. It is vital that your dog is under control when outdoors.

sistent with your recall training. Set your dog up to succeed.

- Fill your treat pouch with extremely tasty rewards. If you have the assis-

tance of a friend, let your dog know that your have the treats by teasing him with one while your friend holds him by the collar.

- Then move across to the other side of the room, open your arms, call his name and then say '**Come**!' or '**Here**!' Your friend should release his collar. As he approaches, keep excited and focused on him to maintain his attention.
- When he arrives hold out the treat for him while gently taking hold of his collar with your other hand. This makes it easier to eventually clip the lead on when you are ending the walk. It's important that your dog is rewarded the **instant** he arrives back by you.

Below: Ask a friend to help by gently holding your dog by his collar while you gain his attention by tempting him with a treat held in your hand.

He knows that you are holding something nice.

*Below: Then back away a short distance, open your arms wide and call '**Come**'. Your friend should let go of his collar so that he can run to you.*

Sound enthusiastic when you call your dog to you.

He should set off towards you eager for the treat.

Food treats can also be used as lures when you are out on a walk.

pull your dog in towards you. The line is to prevent him from moving further away but if you reel him in, he may feel worried and resist. Start moving away, begin to play or create another distraction to encourage him to come back.

Instant Problem Solver

My dog is slow to come back: You should never punish your dog for being slow to return. If you do, he will be even less inclined to return to you the next time you say 'Come'. If he's slow, use a line and practise in quieter areas until he understands what you want.

I'm worried about letting my dog off the lead: If you need extra confidence or worry that your dog will disappear over the horizon when you let him off the lead, you can use a long/trailing line that gives your dog freedom, but restricts how far he can wander off until you are sure that he will respond consistently to your 'Comes'.

• Repeat this game. If possible ask family members to gently restrain your dog while you tease with the treat and rush off into another room before calling him. Extend your practice into your garden.
• Everyone should participate in this game so that he learns that no matter who calls him, it is worth responding.

Above: When training outdoors, consider using a long training line if your dog is not wholly reliable. This enables you to keep him under your control while he still has some freedom to wander and explore.

• If in doubt, use a long training line to give you control while still allowing a great deal of freedom for your dog to play and exercise. However, do not

Below: Keep your focus firmly on your dog and act in an animated way so that he knows that you are really pleased that he is on his way.

This dog is keen and quick to respond – just what a trainer wants.

The pouch holds a supply of treats.

Right: Reward instantly and praise him when he arrives. As he improves, extend the distance and also start to train outside.

TRAINING THE BASIC COMMANDS

Stay

This can be one of the more difficult training commands, especially for young or anxious dogs. However, it is extremely useful and can make many situations safer for you and your dog.

- Begin by facing your dog. Ask him to '**Sit**'.
- In a clear, calm voice raise the palm of your hand (as if indicating 'Stop') and say '**Stay**'. Don't move. After a brief pause 'click' or praise your dog and **instantly** reward. Although you haven't gone anywhere, he needs to learn that remaining in position is what you want from him.

- Repeat this procedure until he is happy to remain in place. If he gets up or moves, then calmly put him back in position. If your dog is particularly busy, then ask a family member or friend to hold his lead, or even attach it to a door handle so that you don't have to chase after him when he fluffs the training.
- Now take a small step backwards after you have given your '**Stay**' command. Then return before he makes a mistake. Repeat and gradually build up the distance you move away. Keeping your focus on your dog will help to prevent him from getting distracted.

- Stay calm until you have returned and don't 'click' or bring out a treat until this point or it is likely that your dog will begin to think about the rewards instead of staying patiently in position.
- It is sensible to introduce a release command which tells your dog he can break away from position. This might be something like '**Free**' or '**OK**'. You can use this at the end of all your training sessions to tell your dog he's free to relax.
- Once he can reliably follow this procedure, begin to turn away from him as you move away. Many dogs make mistakes at this stage so be patient and repeat it as often as necessary. Again, build up the distance you move away. Eventually you should

Give your hand signal and 'click-treat' straight away.

Make sure the hand signal remains clear.

*Don't expect your dog to remain patiently in a **Stay** time after time as you train. He'll need some breaks to recharge.*

To begin with, only move a step or two and then return.

Above: Begin with your dog in a sit position. At this stage you don't move; just reward stillness.

Above: The next stage is to take a small step backwards while you remain facing your dog.

*Above: During the early **Stay** training, release your dog to relax after a few repetitions.*

*Above: You now build on your **Stay** training by turning away from your dog and moving off a few paces.*

be able to walk out of sight while your dog remains in the **Stay**.

- Try to always return to your dog before releasing him since this is the safest method. If your dog is expecting to be released at some point, he may break the **Stay** and perhaps end up in a dangerous situation if you are training outdoors.

Instant Problem Solver

My dog keeps breaking the Stay: This is very likely to happen at some point during training. If it does, just put your dog back in position and begin again. Perhaps don't move so far away this time, so that the temptation to move is not quite so strong. Success in training the **Stay** comes bit by bit.

Don't reprimand your dog if he breaks the Stay and sets off after you. Just patiently go back to the beginning and start again. If it keeps happening, take a break.

Above: This is quite a difficult training exercise for some dogs and it is quite likely that he will break the Stay at some point. If this happens, simply put him back in position and start again.

My dog seems worried: Anxious dogs may find this position hard. Never attempt the **Stay** in any place where he seems frightened. As you progress, ask a friend to hold the lead when you start to practise outside. Never practise off-lead when you are near roads, however.

Instant Training Tip

Avoid telling your dog to '**Stay**' as you leave the house. He is bound to break the **Stay** eventually and this may be detrimental to your overall training success. Instead give your release command just as you close the door so your dog moves after you have given the go-ahead.

Give a clear 'Stay' command before you move away.

Above: Gradually build up the number of steps you take away from your dog over the course of several sessions.

Make your movements calm and any verbal commands even in tone. You do not want to excite the dog and risk him breaking the Stay.

Above: Pause briefly at the furthest extent of your movement before turning back. Over time you will be able to increase both the time and distance.

Don't click too early; you want to be right back at the start point.

*Above: When you do reach your dog, 'click-treat' **instantly** and also reward with praise. Then you can give him a release command.*

GOOD MORNING – TRAINING TIME!

⏱ Instant Training Opportunities During Your Daily Routine

Everyone has slightly different daily routines and requirements. The suggestions outlined in the following chapters cover common training and behavioural issues for which owners commonly request help. Take the suggestions and use them in ways that best benefit your routine and the type of behaviour that your dog displays.

Toilet Training

It is important that when you wake up you let your dog out to toilet **as soon as possible**. Those dogs that have not yet learned to hold on are more likely to have an accident after they have heard you rise and been woken up themselves. With a full bladder, morning accidents are common. By preventing this you will reinforce your dog's habit of toileting in the correct place.

Too Late? If your dog has already toileted then it's not his fault and any attempts to punish him retrospectively won't work. If you do he'll only start to worry when he hears you coming downstairs next time. Put him out and clean up when he's not present. Tonight set your alarm clock for an earlier time and make sure you get up and let him out **before** the accident occurs. You will be able to gradually teach your dog to hold on until morning by pushing the alarm forwards very slightly each time.

Puppy Training If you are trying to train your puppy to toilet outside then getting up early is important. Instead of put-

Left: When you are house-training a young puppy, aim to get into the routine of getting up promptly and going downstairs to let him out to toilet.

⏱ting him outside by himself, go with him so that you can praise him **instantly** for toileting (and check he's actually emptied his bladder rather than just assuming he has). Otherwise you might find that he spends all his time trying to get back in and then has an accident on the floor upon his return. This is just the first outing of many for a puppy owner so leave a coat and shoes by the door alongside some treats and be prepared to go out every hour if you have a young puppy as well as as soon as he wakes, after play time and meal times too. Commit to this and you'll have a house-trained puppy fairly quickly because all his toileting associations are being made in the right place. Don't allow newspapers or pee pads to allow you to become lazy!

Never smack your puppy for toileting indoors

Never smack your puppy for toileting indoors; you will only teach him that sometimes humans are scary and that hands reaching out for them might mean pain.

Never rub your puppy's nose in urine or faeces as punishment. This in no way teaches him better bladder/bowel control or how to ask to go outside, and may cause him to feel anxious around you.

Training Aim

- To praise and reward when he toilets in the right place
- To take your puppy or dog outside before any toileting accidents occur.

Left: Accidents will happen. Don't get cross and reprimand your puppy if things go wrong occasionally. Just clear up and try to be quicker off the mark in future.

Left: Be prepared to accompany your puppy outside to ensure that he has toileted properly. If you put him on the lead, you can keep an eye on what he is doing.

 *Left: As soon as he has relieved himself, praise him and **instantly** give him a treat. You want to establish the connection between toileting outside the house and the provision of a reward.*

Above: Be vigilant and let your puppy out regularly when toilet training.

Below: If you spot your puppy sniffing the floor, act quickly! Usher him outside and treat him if he toilets.

You should start to recognise the body language that means 'I want to go outside'.

51

GOOD MORNING – TRAINING TIME!

Going Back To Bed? You may wish to return to bed after an early morning outing. Puppies and energetic dogs may be charged up and ready to play, making settling down again difficult for them. Ensure you provide an interesting toy or large chew before you go back to bed. Otherwise he may bark or cry to get you to come back or he may get into other trouble while unsupervised. Of course, these are also useful distractions while you're getting ready or taking a shower. Make this provision **before** your dog learns bad habits.

Training Aim
Offer the activity after the dog has toileted outside and before you leave him again in his resting area.

Breakfast's Up
Start the day in the right way. Weigh out your dog's breakfast, pour it into his bowl and ask him to '**Sit**' before leaning down to put the bowl on the floor. If he gets up before you've put it down, then stand up again so the bowl is removed from his reach. Ask him to '**Sit**' once more and then try again. Repeat until he remains sitting until the bowl touches the floor. Then

Make sure that your dog has something to occupy him and that he is kept in a safe, doggy-proofed area

instantly give a release command such as '**OK**' or '**Take it**' to signal that he can go ahead and eat. Stay calm and patient while you practise this task. If you get frustrated or angry, your dog will begin to get worried too and his behaviour at meal times may become problematic. For a more exciting breakfast routine for your dog see Morning Mayhem (opposite page).

If you haven't taught the 'Sit' command yet, then use your dog's breakfast to do so before trying this technique.

Training Aim
Praise your dog verbally while he remains in the sitting position, waiting for your release signal.

Measure out the food allowance while the dog is in a Sit.

Left and below: Breakfast is a good time to teach your dog to 'Sit' patiently and wait for his morning food ration to arrive.

Don't put the bowl down if your dog moves out of the Sit.

Morning Mayhem

Most family homes are pretty hectic in the mornings. Everyone is rushing around trying to get ready for school and work and sometimes the dog ends up attention-seeking, getting under people's feet or getting into things he shouldn't. This is particularly difficult when you own a young dog or puppy as they have recharged their batteries all night and are normally raring to go in the morning.

Prevent this by making sure that your dog has something to occupy him and that he is kept in a safe, doggy-proofed area. Pour your dog's break- fast kibble into an activity ball so that he can spend time rolling it around to get at his first meal of the day. This is best done in an area where he is not likely to get in the way of family rushing around trying to get ready. You may find that clever positioning of a dog gate will allow you to keep your dog safely out of the way at this busy time.

Training Aim

Encourage your dog to play by himself before he has a chance to get under your feet.

Left: One way to keep a puppy or young dog out of mischief in the morning is to give him his breakfast kibble inside an activity ball, He'll have to work hard to get it to drop out of the ball.

Below: Bend down and put the breakfast bowl on the floor, but keep your training focus and maintain control by asking your dog to wait before he can have it.

*Below: When the bowl is safely on the floor and your dog has not made any rushed move to get at it, **instantly** give a release command so that he can go ahead and enjoy his food.*

Above: Very young puppies may eat up to four or five times a day. They need to fuel their rapid growth.

*The hand gesture backs up the **Wait** command.*

*'**Take it**' means that it is fine for the dog to start eating.*

Once he's started, let him enjoy his breakfast without interruption or other distraction.

GOOD MORNING – TRAINING TIME!

Slipper Chasing

Puppies often love chasing slippers or dressing gown cords when their owners are rushing around in the morning. To reduce this or prevent it, make sure that you

Above: Some puppies just love chasing shoes and slippers. But even though they look cute, don't indulge them.

never make a game out of chasing feet and don't participate in tuggy games with sleeves or cords.

Instead, the moment your puppy starts this game, or even better if you see him about to start it, stand still and wait. Never kick out at him. This game is more fun for the dog if both sides join in and so your puppy will stop once he realises that it's all one-sided. The **instant** he does so, 'click-treat' or praise him and then redirect his attention onto his own toys or scatter some tiny treats onto the floor to keep him busy while you continue doing what you were doing. The sooner you teach him to play a desirable game, the less established this will become.

Above: You can redirect your dog's attention onto a colourful toy if he is inclined to tug at your clothing or chase your slippered feet.

Instant Training Tip If your puppy always wants to start this game as you greet him, then arrive in the room prepared with a large, dangly toy to redirect his focus. Leave this toy on the stairs or just outside the room so you can pick it up before you enter.

Training Aim

- Watch your dog's body language to see if he's shaping up to chase your clothing, and pre-empt this game whenever possible.

It's tempting to tug the cord free, but this isn't to be recommended.

He's probably hoping for a tug-of-war.

Above: The golden rule in this situation is don't start a tugging match. If you refuse to join in, the game will no longer seem rewarding.

- Stop moving immediately when chasing or tugging begins.
- Re-direct the dog to an appropriate game.

Dog Gate

Dogs can easily rush out through the open door when the children are putting their coats and shoes on and checking their bags before setting off for school. Keep your dog behind a dog gate or in another room if your door leads out to an insecure yard or a dangerous road. Dogs should never be trusted to remain safely inside. A dog gate is very useful on many occasions when time for training is short.

Left: If you think that there is a danger that your dog may rush outside when family members are leaving for work or school, confine him safely behind a dog gate with a food-charged activity toy to occupy his attention.

*Right: 'Click-treat' and praise your dog the **instant** he stops tugging on the cord.*

Scatter some tiny treats onto the floor to keep him busy

Right: Don't join in the game. Stand still and wait for him to dop the cord

A few treats thrown on the floor will keep him occupied.

TRAINING WHEN OUT FOR A WALK

Collar Fitting

Before you take your dog out he should be fitted with a strong, secure collar. Check that the collar is not fastened too tightly – you should be able to fit two fingers between his neck and the fastenened collar. Check this regularly. The collar should include a name tag with your contact telephone number and address indelibly marked on it.

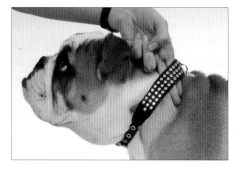

Left: Check the fit of your dog's collar regularly. You should be able to slip two fingers easily into the fastened collar.

Get Ready

Quietly prepare the items you need for the walk. Once these things have been gathered together, you will have them to hand each day when you need them. A large treat pouch can hold poo bags, whistles, toy/ball, clickers, as well as treats.

Try not to excite your dog by deliberately teasing or verbally encouraging anticipation of the walk before you are completely ready to leave the house. Doing so will only make it more likely that he will leap around and be difficult to handle as you walk out of the door. It also makes him more likely to pull on the lead when the walk begins.

When you're ready, pick up the lead and call your dog to you and ask him to '**Sit**'. He might be very excited when he sees you holding the lead and will probably rush around grabbing toys,

jumping up or barking, so you must remain calm and patient. Stand still and wait. After some bouncing and exuberant reactions, he will eventually begin to realise that nothing is happening and should then focus his attention on you. Ask him again to '**Sit**'. When he does, clip the lead to his collar (avoid attaching to the ring of the name tag as this is not strong enough) and then **instantly** '**click-treat**' or **praise** him. Giving up a few minutes at the start of the walk to wait for calmer behaviour will help in the longer term. Although he won't be perfect straight away, each time you wait will make it easier.

If your dog is particularly badly behaved when the lead comes out, you have the option of putting the lead down and walking away, ignoring him completely. Try again after five to ten minutes. With experience he should learn that his current behaviour is not resulting in the expected walk. When he is calmer you can quietly clip the lead on and go out, so teaching him that this response is more successful.

Instant Training Tip Never chase your dog to try to clip the lead on. This may be perceived as a fun game which he tries every time. Imagine how you would like your dog to behave at the door and try to set up the situation so that this, or something similar, occurs consistently.

Training Aim

Attach the lead and leave the house only when your dog shows signs of being calm.

Left: It is helpful to have all the things that you are likely to need on a walk – poo bags, treats, clicker, toys, whistle etc. – stashed ready in a treat pouch before you set off.

Right: Don't attempt to clip on the lead if your dog leaps around in a frenzy at the sight of it. Only good behaviour should result in the walk getting under way.

Right: Training two dogs at once isn't easy. You'll probably make more progress with individual lessons initially.

Have your 'props' ready in your pouch.

Multiple Dogs? If you own more than one dog then you'll have to approach their training individually; especially if one is worse than the other. One-to-one sessions usually speed up the dogs' progress. Once you've been successful, you can bring the dogs together for joint training. Indicate which dog you are referring to each time by saying its name before the command.

*Right: Stand still, avoid eye contact and wait for the dog to calm down. When he is paying attention to you, ask him to '**Sit**'.*

Below: When he sits obediently, you are ready to clip on the lead. Make sure that you attach it to the proper collar ring, not the clasp of the name tag which is too flimsy.

*Below: When the lead is on and the dog is still sitting calmly, **instantly** 'click-treat' and tell him he is a 'Good boy'.*

Jumping around – ignored. Sitting – treated. Lesson learned!

TRAINING WHEN OUT FOR A WALK

Heelwork

Dogs are not born knowing that humans like them to walk next to them on a loose lead. You need to teach your dog that this is a good idea and these lessons will take commitment and patience to teach effectively.

While it is good practice always to insist upon good heelwork, this is harder to achieve if your dog hasn't been exercised that day. If possible, drive to the park and let him run and play and then start training. This won't be a permanent routine but it will reduce the chances of bad habits developing as he surges forwards to get to the park in as little time as possible.

To practise heelwork, start with you dog sitting beside you. Get his attention and while he is focused on you, move forward one step. If he walks with you, say 'Heel' and reward him instantly before moving on a few paces. Keep praising your dog while the lead remains relaxed. Keep the treat ready to offer but be careful not to encourage jumping. Gradually build up the distance your dog walks beside you before you offer the reward.

Pay Attention! While walking your dog you should pay attention to him and resist chatting on your mobile or indulging in other distractions. If your attention is diverted you will not be in a position to reward the correct behaviours instantly, or spot when your dog is feeling worried (perhaps by traffic, people or dogs). You will also make it much more likely that your dog will begin to focus on other more interesting events going on around him. This will almost certainly result in more pulling and lack of focus on you.

Left: Once your dog has let off a bit of steam by running and playing when you get to the park, you are ready to practise heelwork. Reattach the lead and ask him to 'Sit' at your side.

Right: Say his name to attract his attention and then take a step or two forwards. If he walks by your side, say 'Heel' and then instantly 'click-treat' and praise him.

You are looking for a nice relaxed lead during heelwork.

To encourage the right heelwork behaviour you should:

- 'Click-treat' and praise each time your dog turns to look back at you while walking.
- 'Click-treat' or praise every time you feel the lead going slack.

The dog is pulling ahead now, causing the lead to go taut.

Use an animated tone of voice to call his name.

Above: If the dogs pulls, stop. You mustn't tolerate being dragged along.

Above: When he turns to see what's going on, lure him back to you with a treat held down low to entice him.

Above: Begin to walk again. If he stays by your side, 'click-treat' and praise. Treats come when he's at your heel.

Bend down to offer the treat with a small dog to avoid any jumping.

Drive to the park and let him run and play and then start training

- When your dog pulls, instantly stop. Pulling should never be a successful behaviour. Lure him back by your side and continue walking. 'Click-treat' while you are walking so he learns that walking by your side earns the reward.
- Avoid getting into a 'You pull so I pull' pattern by resisting pulling the lead tight to counteract your dog. If your dog feels tension in the lead, he will automatically pull against it.
- **Only offer treats and praise when the lead is loose**. Be aware of your timing since if you offer a treat when he pulls (to try to encourage him not to do that again), he might learn to surge forwards and then come back for his reward. The same applies to the timing of your '**Good dog**' praise. Make sure he is actually doing the correct action before you say it.
- If your dog is poor at heelwork then begin with **very short sessions.** Just focus on walking a little way and then back again. As he improves, gradually build up the distance.

Instant Training Tip Avoid shouting '**Heel**' every time your dog pulls ahead. Unless you have already taught him that '**Heel**' is associated with walking next to you on a loose lead, it will begin to mean '**Pull**'; completely the opposite command! Your timing is therefore very important.

59

TRAINING WHEN OUT FOR A WALK

Large or Strong Dog? Sometimes we need a little more control than a regular collar and lead allow. Although you will still need to follow the training instructions to reward your dog for focusing on you and whenever the lead is slack, there are training tools that make this more likely. Try a well-fitted headcollar or training harness. These act by helping you to guide your dog more easily, to reduce his ability to pull directly forwards and make it safer to

Right: A headcollar discourages a dog from pulling by steering his head around when he pulls the lead taut.

Below: A double-ended lead gives extra control over powerful dogs.

walk by busy roads. Additional control can be obtained by using a double-ended lead which is a lead with trigger clips at either end. This allows you to attach one to the headcollar or the harness and the other to the collar. This makes 'steering' your dog or reducing lunging easier to achieve.

Above: A training harness fits around a dog's body with straps that extend under his front legs. Surging ahead is dissuaded because the harness tightens as the dog pulls.

Walking with a Pushchair

If you own a strong dog and need to walk him alongside a pushchair, a headcollar or harness may be helpful. Alternatively, a waist belt can give you a secure attachment point for the lead and eliminate the risk that the dog could pull on the hand holding the lead and so accidentally drag the pushchair into danger.

If your dog is reactive towards other dogs, then it is sensible to engage the pushchair's brake when you see another dog approaching. Step away from the pushchair so that no possible dog-on-dog reaction could tip it over or involve a dog getting near to the baby. Get your dog's attention and reward him for keeping that focus while the other dog passes by.

Sit And Wait Before Crossing Set a pattern whereby your dog pauses before each crossing to sit and wait for your signal to cross. This is a nice training technique but also **might** mean he will pause if one day he breaks loose and reaches a road without you. That pause may be just enough to allow drivers time to see him and brake.

Above: If you need to keep both hands free, such as when you are pushing a baby's buggy, a waist belt allows you to attach the lead to a secure clip on the belt.

Left: Both hands can hold on to and steer the buggy while your dog is securely attached to your waist belt.

Right: If you sense that your dog might start to react towards another dog that is approaching, stop the buggy, step away and try to hold his focus.

Right: Reward him with a treat if he keeps his eyes on you and ignores the passing dog.

The baby is safely strapped in and out of harm's way .

Large dogs, like this Akita, are immensely powerful. He could topple the buggy over if he were to pull suddenly on your guiding hand.

Engage the brake if you need to step away from the buggy.

TRAINING WHEN OUT FOR A WALK

Driving With Your Dog

It is often necessary to drive to a good walking location and many owners use this as an excuse not to work on their lead-walking skills. Although you may not need it often, when you do require good heelwork it is nice to have some control. Practise your **'Sit'** command as you leave the house, and to add an extra moment of control before you ask your dog to jump into the car. This will make it easier to manage your dog during vet clinic visits or if your dog is ever prescribed a regime of restricted exercise on a lead, such as after an operation or illness.

> ### Your dog should always be secure when he travels

Noisy Traveller Driving with dogs can be a real headache. Many dogs become vocal when in the car. This may mean your dog is not relaxed with the travelling process, is worried by something outside the car, or that he is overly excited. Try to observe when the problem begins, how he is behaving and whether he will respond to your training commands.

Your dog should always be secure when he travels. Many owners successfully use an internal car crate. This is a secure den in which your dog can

travel in safety. It prevents him from moving about in the car, darting out when the door is opened and generally provides extra security. Make this area more enticing by scattering treats in the blanket, providing him with a toy and even consider draping the crate with a blanket as you are driving to remove any external visual stimuli that may be arousing him.

An alternative to the crate is a car harness. This is a specially designed

Left: A car harness allows you to secure your dog to the car's own seatbelt fittings.

*Above: Ask your dog to **'Sit'** before letting him jump into the car. It helps to reinforce your instant training regime.*

Above: A car crate provides an excellent solution to the problem of keeping a dog safe and secure in the rear of the car while you are driving.

This chewy toy can be stuffed with treats.

Above: Old or injured dogs may need a car ramp to get in and out.

*Below: We've all seen it, but this is **not** the way to travel with a dog in the car. It's distracting and potentially dangerous for the dog.*

harness which attaches to a seatbelt. It is advisable to get your dog used to wearing the harness before you put him in the car. Make sure the harness is fitted correctly or he may wriggle free while you are driving.

'Good Dog' Whenever your dog is travelling in the car, remember that he still needs to be encouraged to behave appropriately. Praise him and even ask your passengers to offer rewards when

Above: If you are planning a long journey, it can pay to put a food-filled toy in the car crate to keep your dog mentally stimulated and happy while the miles roll by.

he is quiet and settled. Shouting at him when he barks will only make it seem as if you are joining in, so resist this temptation!

CHAPTER 6

TRAINING WHEN OUT FOR A WALK

We're Here!

If your dog barks through excitement when he arrives at the place where you are going to have your walk, then remain sitting in the car. When he pauses, **instantly** 'click-treat' and open your door and get out. If you cannot bear sitting in the car with a noisy dog, or if he resumes barking when you get out, stand by the car, facing away from your dog and wait

Above: Don't open the rear door if your dog is barking excitedly in anticipation of the walk. Only quiet behaviour should be rewarded.

for a moment of quiet before you open the door. Your dog should learn that calm quiet behaviour results in the walk beginning, while noisy, excitable behaviour delays its onset. Remember that dogs should not be left for long in

Please be a responsible dog owner; pay attention and pick up after your pet

hot cars, so make sure that you park in the shade with windows open while you work on this aspect of his training.

Instant Training Advice If your dog gets over-excited in this way, reduce excitement levels at the beginning of the walk by including some on-lead training for the first five or ten minutes before letting him off.

Nervous puppies and dogs will often take longer to adjust to car travel, especially if they are worried by some of the experiences during the walk. If meeting strangers or other dogs when out walking worry your dog, then he may begin to feel anxious when he gets into the car as he is anticipating such a meeting. Try to arrange trips to quiet places or to meet friendly, familiar people instead until his confidence levels build up sufficiently.

Above: It is very anti-social to leave your dog's faeces lying as a hazard for other unwary park visitors. Pick it up in a bag and dispose of it.

Running Free!

When you arrive at the park it's tempting to immediately let your dog off the lead while you walk around chatting or just doing your own thing. Before you do, consider other walkers and their pets who may not want an unsupervised dog rushing around near them. If you are not paying attention, then you won't be able to pick up after your dog has defecated which is a violation of the law and the reason why many public areas have banned dogs. Please be a responsible dog owner; pay attention and pick up after your pet.

When you arrive at the park or open space, it is a good idea to continue your on-lead training for a few minutes. Then, when you feel the time is appropriate, ask your dog to '**Sit**'. Unclip his lead *(right)* while keeping one hand on his collar to prevent him from running off. Slowly release your hold and say '**Off you go**' to tell him he is free to go and play.

If your dog has not learned to come back yet or has a history of running away to pester dogs or people, then you should use a **long training line**. This will instantly prevent him from run-

ning off while you continue training him. If he won't willingly return, **don't drag him** towards you as he will feel stressed and be less likely to want to come close. Instead hold the line and play a game with a toy by yourself, feign interest in something on the ground or in your treat pouch or begin to walk in another direction. When your dog chooses to approach, **praise** him so he knows this was a good choice.

Continue the training by showing

him a really tasty treat but don't feed it to him. Wait a few minutes until he is focusing on something else, perhaps sniffing the grass, and then call him in your happy, excited voice and immediately offer him the reward for getting it right this time.

Instant Training Tip If your dog has known aggressive tendencies please keep him on a lead. If using a longer line you must avoid any danger of it getting tangled around other people or their dogs.

Left: A long training line gives you a very welcome extra element of control when you are training a dog whose recall is not completely reliable. You can even use your foot as a way of restricting how much 'play' you allow in the line.

Choose a toy that your dog loves playing with.

*Below: When he's back at your side and focusing on you, the trainer, praise him for being a '**Good boy**'. Now show him a treat but withhold it for the time being. You want to 'click-treat' the correct recall response, so wait a few moments and then call him back when he's nosing around elsewhere. If he comes willingly this time, 'click-treat'.*

Above: It's important that you don't use the line as a way to simply drag your dog back to you. Instead, call him and entice him back with a toy or the promise of a treat. You want to reward willingness to return.

Take care that the extra line does get tangled around your ankles.

TRAINING WHEN OUT FOR A WALK

If your dog likes excitement, then you have to become exciting to be with. Use an excited voice, become animated as he runs towards you and if he's less interested in food bring out a favourite toy and play with him. Run in different directions to tempt him to follow you. If you're walking with a family member, then play a game where you each call your dog between you or hide behind trees *(right)* and then call his name so that he has to seek you out in turn.

Left: Make recall training fun. Run in the other direction or dash off to hide.

Rover Come! Rover Come! Rover!!

Don't get into the bad habit of calling and calling your dog repeatedly in the forlorn hope that he will eventually pay attention. If he's ignoring you because he's doing something more exciting, then you're just wasting your time and actually teaching him to ignore your call. Begin recall training in areas where there are fewer distractions to tempt him and only start to try the recall in more challenging situations where there are more plentiful and varied distractions when he is reliable elsewhere.

He should enjoy an active hide and seek game.

⏱ Instant Training Tip

If your dog likes squeaky sounds, then carry a squeaky toy in your pocket for emergencies. If he is distracted and you need him to respond quickly try giving a couple of quick squeaks of the toy. The **second** he looks up, act in an excited way and even rush off in another direction. Most dogs will come running to join in your fun game. Try not to overuse this technique, however, or it will lose effectiveness.

Below: For emergency use, it can pay to keep a favourite squeaky toy in your pocket. If your dog hares off in the opposite direction and you must get him back quickly, take out the toy and squeak it loudly once or twice.

Whistle Training

Some people find using a whistle a very helpful way to improve their recall training. However, your dog won't automatically know what the whistle sound means, so you will have to train him to pair the noise with rewards.

• Begin this work at home where there are only a few distractions.

• Prepare with your treat pouch or your dog's meal ready to offer. Get your

Below: You begin whistle training by pairing the sound of the whistle with the arrival of food. ⏱

Pick a toy that is robust and which emits quite a loud squeak that will carry a fair distance.

Right: As soon as spots you, turn and run in the other direction. He should come dashing after you to collect the toy. You're back in control.

• Fit in 'whistle training' sessions when you have a few minutes to spare during the day or just prior to your dog's meal times when you're offering him food anyway. The more time you spend pairing up the sound and the rewards, the more reliable his response will be.

Instant Training Tip

Avoid blowing the whistle too hard while indoors since it may be very loud and off-putting for your dog. Keep it away from children who may be tempted to blow it far too often and so reduce its effectiveness around the dog.

dog's attention and then peep the whistle while **instantly** offering a piece of a treat or some kibble. Repeat several times.

• Then ask another person to hold your dog at the other end of the room. Tease him with a treat and rush away. The helper should be ready to release your dog as soon as you blow the whistle. Use lots of enthusiasm when he responds well and reward him when he arrives. Practise around your home and garden and then try this on walks.

Below: The next step is to ask a helper to hold your dog while you rush backwards tempting him with a treat. When you blow the whistle, the helper should release the dog.

Keep the treat hand extended offering a tasty reward.

He'll be eager to come to you.

*Below: Reward him the **instant** he arrives. A connection has now been established between the sound of a whistle, the act of running to you and the provision of a treat. Keep practising to build on your success.*

'Good boy – treat time.'

TRAINING WHEN OUT FOR A WALK

Social Etiquette

We consider it very good manners for a dog to '**Sit**' when greeting a person. Since dogs don't automatically know this rule, you must reinforce it as often as possible. Teach the '**Sit**' command at home and then begin practising outside. Ask people to wait until your puppy or dog is sitting before they offer a treat or crouch down to say hello. We all know dog-friendly people who don't mind when the dog jumps up to say hello. The problem is that other people do mind and this can be the cause for complaint if your dog accidentally scratches or bruises them, knocks them over or just marks their clothes with muddy paws. It is good practice

> We consider it very good manners for a dog to 'Sit' when greeting a person

to ask your dog to sit even if you are talking to a person who is not interested in him.

Every time your friends visit or when you meet other dog owners, ask them to help you practise the approach and '**Sit**' technique. If your dog has plenty of practice at doing this, he is more likely to do it again with a new person in the future.

*Above: Dogs should learn good manners too. Ask your dog to '**Sit**' when you greet someone.*

Instant Training Tip If your dog is too excited and won't '**Sit**', **walk him away** and get his focus back on you. Practise a few '**Sits**' and reward him really well so that he remembers that this is worth doing. Then approach and try again. Make sure the visitor stays calm and doesn't interact with the dog at first so that he has a chance to succeed.

Muddy Paws

After your walk your dog may have muddy paws or a muddy body. It is a good idea to get him used to being wiped/dried off even if you currently use an old car or have an old carpet on which a few paw prints don't matter. Think about the future when you buy a nice new carpet or when your dog is

Above: The other person should only pat and acknowledge the dog if he's remained sitting.

being looked after by a friend while you're away. Having clean paws then may be essential.

Keep a couple of old towels in your car or near to the door where you can reach them without letting your dog

*Above: To accustom a dog to towelling, touch the back of one leg and **instantly** 'click-treat' when he lifts his paw.*

trail muddy prints through your home.

Calmly ask your dog to '**Stand**' and then gently touch the back of one leg to encourage your dog to lift his paw. **Instantly** '**click-treat**' so he learns that this is a worthwhile response. Gently dry the paw with the towel and '**click-treat**' **again**. It can be helpful if two of you can practise this; one towels while the other 'click-treats' to get things started. If your dog has sensitive paws then you will need to spend longer associating your touch with the arrival of rewards. Do this by touching the paw briefly and offering the 'click-treat'. Build up the time you hold the paw before the 'click' occurs. Stay calm and steadily work on each paw thoroughly, praising and rewarding as you go. Work on each paw to ensure he tolerates all four being handled equally well.

Left: Some dogs, notably spaniels, never seem happier than when they are cavorting around in the mud or launching themselves into puddles and streams. It's fun to watch but a challenge to clean. That's when a bit of towel training will stand you in good stead.

If your dog is very sensitive to being towelled or gets particularly dirty, you might consider fitting protective covers in your car and then allow him to dry off in a non-carpeted area, or within his familiar indoor kennel, at home.

Your dog may be very wet if it has been raining while you were walking. While most will learn to enjoy being towelled down from head to toe, some dogs worry if the towel is put over their head so take this part slowly. Make sure your dog has fun – this needn't be a chore at the end of the walk. See it as a final game instead. And yes, you probably will end up a little wet and muddy too!

A brisk towelling is an extremely effective way to dry a wet dog.

Above: Once he is used to lifting his paw on demand, introduce the towel to the routine. Keep treating if he remains quiet and doesn't struggle.

Above: The next stage is to get your dog used to having his whole body towelled down. Take care around the head and ears.

Above: Continue to reinforce your dog's habit of standing still while you dry him so that good habits can become established.

HOME ALONE TRAINING

Leaving your dog alone at home is something that most dog owners have to do at some point. Unfortunately, this is a time when lots of mishaps can occur so it's important to plan ahead.

Planning For Your Absence

Where to leave your dog is a concern to owners of puppies or dogs that have already displayed chewing or separation anxiety problems. Every home is different. The area in which you leave your dog should be safe and secure. Put all small items away, clear counters of all tempting objects and cover electric cables with protective covers. Look around and try to imagine what your dog may get up to while you're away. If you don't have a secure area and your dog is likely to get up to mischief, then you should consider using a large indoor kennel, or a dog pen. Both should be areas where your dog likes to spend time so encourage him to go in there while you are at home too. Areas away from windows or glass doors are preferable if your dog barks at passers-by.

Above: While a kitchen or utility room may seem an ideal place to leave a dog alone in the house, if it also contains a washing machine that you are planning to run or a refrigerator with a noisy, gurgling compressor, he may find it a rather alarming environment. Perhaps think again.

Your dog needs a comfortable place to rest as well as plenty of choices of playthings

Left: Large dog pens equipped with comfortable bedding and toys offer a secure area for your dog to stay out of mischief while you are out of the house.

Right: Picture windows and glass doors offer a dog a great view of the world outside. However, if he's liable to bark at passers-by, keep them off limits.

Try not to leave your dog in a confined space while washing machines, dishwashers or other appliances are running. These often emit beeps, motor noise and other sounds that can worry a dog and cause him to try to escape. He may even develop sound sensitivity.
The tone of the alarms that warn us to come back and switch off the appliance are designed to gain our attention and this can be particularly intensive for our dogs which have an excellent sense of hearing.

What to leave behind for your dog is very important. Many people leave their dog in a utility room or kitchen area since these places are often the least vulnerable to damage. However, they are also fairly uninteresting rooms unless you go to some effort to make them more appealing. Imagine how you would feel if you had to spend the entire day in a small area without anything to do. Then think about how your behaviour would change when you finally got out of that space and had some company. You'd want to burn off energy, socialise, eat and chat as a form of compensation. You might also be in a bad mood as a result of the day's frustrations. Although we advise people not to assume that their dog feels as they do, in this case it is a

Left: Dogs that are left alone with little in the way of stimulation to divert them can develop problems such as chewing and destructive behaviour.

helpful way to understand how your dog might react after being left alone with nothing to do.

Your dog needs a comfortable place to rest as well as plenty of choices of playthings. Boredom is a big problem and can lead to barking and chewing problems. Most toy manufacturers advise owner supervision while the dog plays, but once you know your dog's style of play, you may be able to safely leave him with certain toys and edible items. Larger activity toys and substantial chews are often perfectly suitable since they are unlikely to be accidentally swallowed.

Instant Training Tip You should try to prepare a stuffed activity toy in advance so that you always have one to hand, even when you have to rush out unexpectedly.

Right: A comfortable place that the dog recognises as his own is vital. But it is unlikely that he will sleep for the whole day, so plan to leave some safe toys as well, such as large chews and activity toys that will not crack and splinter.

HOME ALONE TRAINING

When you will return should also be considered. If you are going to be away for longer than five hours, or if your dog just cannot cope with being alone for extended periods or has not yet learned to be toilet-trained to that extent, then arrange for a neighbour, family member or a dog walker to come in and let your dog out.

How you respond when you leave and return can have a big impact upon your dog's behaviour. Avoid great big goodbyes as you will only draw attention to the fact that you are going to leave your dog alone. By offering lots of attention before you go, you will emphasise the contrast between the time when you are there and when you are not. Make sure that you have left a bowl of water and your dog's toys in an accessible place and then calmly leave without any fuss.

It's probably not necessary for all owners to ignore their pets for great lengths of time when they return but if your dog is particularly enthusiastic or has some over-attachment issues then it is better to tone down hellos when you return. Try to avoid greeting your dog

until you have taken off your coat and got properly inside. It may help to ask him to go fetch a specific toy so that he has a 'job' to do before you greet and pet him. Wait for him to calm a little before doing this. Over time his response should gradually become more manageable and you'll probably find he goes to find his toy before coming to say 'Hello'.

Problem Solving

Oops So you've returned to some level of destruction? Your **immediate response** is important here and so you'll need lots of self-control. You may feel angry but getting cross and punishing your dog won't make

Below: Take time before you go out to prepare for your absence. Make sure that the water bowl is full, the bed is ready and there are toys available.

This ball will slowly release treats as it rolls around.

Below: When you are ready to go, simply put on your coat and leave the house with a minimum of fuss. Hopefully he'll be nosing around his toys like this, or settling down on his bed for a snooze.

things any better. In fact it is likely that you'll increase the problem as your dog can become anxious as he begins to anticipate your return and this may then lead to him developing toileting or chewing problems.

Take a deep breath and don't react! If possible let your dog out into the garden or into another room while you take a moment to assess the damage. What has he focused on?

Has he stolen something edible? In this case try to leave him with several different stuffed food toys when you go out next time. Secure the bin and consider child locks on your cupboards or fridge if his talent is in breaking into these areas.

Has he damaged something belonging to you or the area around the door or window? In this case he may have an over-attachment problem or something is causing him to feel fearful while he is inside, provoking an escape response. In that case you will need to address his underlying anxiety. Your vet will be able to refer you to a qualified canine behaviour specialist.

Has he chewed apparently random objects in different locations? In this case, chances are that he was bored and so you must make sure

Above: Don't blow your top if you come home to find that something has been chewed to pieces. The dog will not associate your anger with the incident that aroused it.

that he has things to do and that he receives exercise before you leave him. A dog-walker may help you to avoid further bad habits by breaking up the day for you and tiring out your dog through exercise into the bargain.

Instant Training Tip

Dog pheromone therapy products can help to relax your dog while he is alone and this is something you can install quickly and easily. These products are synthetic copies of the naturally appeasing pheromones that are produced by a lactating bitch. They have a calming effect on puppies and mature dogs that are stressed and can help in reducing anxiety-related destructive behaviour. They come in a diffuser form that plugs into an electrical socket and slowly releases the pheromone into the dog's home environment, or as a pump spray which can be used inside a car or travel crate or wherever else it might be appropriate.

Below: When you come home later on, again keep your responses low key. Avoid exciting your dog with big hellos; instead just come in calmly and aim to take off your coat and put down your things before you give the dog your attention.

Below: Don't respond to attention-seeking behaviour like jumping at your legs and barking. The dog must not come to think that the reward of your greeting can always be elicited by pestering and jumping up.

This is not a reaction you want to foster.

Below: When you are ready, you can greet him and show him how glad you are to see him again. You are not being unaffectionate by managing your greeting in this way; instead you are establishing a routine that makes life more harmonious for both of you.

'Yes, I've missed you too, but I'm home now and we can play.'

TRAINING AT PLAY TIME!

Play time should be fun and entertaining. While play is a natural instinct in dogs that have been able to explore and express themselves as youngsters, they don't automatically know the rules of each game that we humans devise.

Regular Play

You should try to fit in some play time as often as possible. Play is a great way to help your dog wind down after a challenging training session or after he has been particularly well behaved. Play should be fun for all concerned and will help your dog to bond with you.

The type of dog and his temperament will shape the types of games that will interest him. Take time to learn about your dog's natural breed instincts and then think about what games might be interesting to him and which ones would be useful on a day-to-day basis.

Left: Play can range from a simple game with a ball or a toy to fully fledged trick-training involving a range of props. It all depends on how much time and effort you are prepared to put in.

Play should have structure and some established rules since an excited dog can potentially cause injury or frighten someone if they play roughly or accidentally mouth or jump up onto a person. Dogs have a

Play should be fun and will help your dog to bond with you

Not all dogs enjoy this type of physical tussling.

Above and left: Youngsters like to play energetically with the family dog, but it can lead to bad habits developing. Certainly you must put a stop to any nipping of hands or faces; that could lead to a nasty accident.

hard time interpreting what we want from play time. Often one member of the family will enjoy calm, structured play while another gets down onto the floor and wrestles with the dog. If this sort of rough-and-tumble game is directed towards the wrong person, it becomes a potential disaster.

Go back to your list of family House Rules and decide which behaviours you want to encourage and which ones are less appropriate. Your dog's physical fitness will also influence which games you should and should not consider. Your list may include:

• **Never encourage play biting on face, hands or feet.** Any game that teaches your dog to mouth on bodies or clothing really is an accident waiting to happen. Your dog may have fantastic bite inhibition (knowledge of how gently to apply teeth to avoid causing injury or anger in you or another dog), but if he chooses to play with a stranger or a young child then the results could be catastrophic. If your puppy or

If this puppy bites too hard, he'll soon learn about it!

Above: Don't get involved in games of tug if you don't want them to happen. If your dog is resisting giving up a toy, you must teach him to swap it for something else, not drag it from his grasp by sheer force.

Left: Puppies learn bite inhibition – how much bite pressure is tolerated in a game – through rough-and-tumble play with their littermates.

dog takes hold of you or your clothing during play, then you should **instantly** stop the game. Calmly remove yourself from the area to show him that the consequence of this action was that the game ended. You have to **react instantly** for your dog to understand this concept. If you can sense that he is tempted to grab, then redirect his attention onto a toy instead and praise him for playing that game.

• **Don't play tuggy unless you mean to.** Playing a tuggy game is usually completely fine as long as this is not occurring when you try to take away something your dog has stolen or when you are playing Fetch and want him to give up the toy. You will need to work hard to train your dog to swap instead. If he starts to tug then keep your hand still and close to your body. This will reduce the excitement and make it more likely that he will let go. You should praise him for letting go.

TRAINING AT PLAY TIME!

• **Child-dog play must be supervised.** Children must never be allowed to physically wrestle or restrain a dog and should not be encouraged to lift and carry small dogs around. By teaching your children how to play properly and how to respect your dog's own space it is likely that many problems can be avoided. Remember that children

Left: The dog is not amused… children often don't pick up when a dog's body language signals discontent.

Children must never be allowed to physically wrestle or restrain a dog

are poor at recognising canine signals and so it's your duty to make sure things remain calm and controlled. It is normal for your dog to play using his mouth but human skin and faces are very easily damaged if your dog makes a mistake. Just as child-child play

often ends in tears, dogs also may get over-aroused and make mistakes. Unfortunately, whereas children hit or kick one another, a dog naturally corrects his playmate by grabbing the muzzle. You must therefore interrupt the game before this happens. Encourage structured '**Fetch**' and trick games instead.

Fetch It!

Some dogs will naturally chase a moving toy and bring it back to you but most need a little encouragement to ensure that this happens reliably and without tension. You can teach this inside or even while in the garden hanging out washing on the line.

• Prepare with some toys that your dog likes but doesn't try to protect from you. If he has already learned to rush away with a toy, then clip his long line to his collar so that this is no longer an option.
• Start by teasing your dog a little with the toy and then toss it a short distance or roll it along the floor.
• When your dog picks it up offer praise and then respond in an excited manner to make him want to rush back to you.

Initially just toss it a few feet away so that your dog can get the hang of the game.

*As your dog grabs the toy you should call encouragement, '**Good dog!**', and behave excitely which should stimulate him to run back to you holding the toy.*

• The timing of rewards in this game is critical. If you offer treats too early, your dog will probably drop the toy on his way back to you. If you don't reward when he gets to you, he may soon learn not to bother.
• Never grab at the toy. Instead offer him a tasty treat from one hand while

Pick a favourite toy for this game – one that your dog will want to chase.

Left: When playing Fetch It!, don't make the mistake of throwing the toy a long way if you are playing with a puppy who is still quite small. You can begin by rolling a ball or tossing a toy just a short distance.

The timing of rewards in this game is critical

*Below: Try to present your reward only once he has returned, as many dogs will drop the toy as soon as they spot the treat that you are offering. Avoid grabbing the toy from your dog's mouth. Take a moment to praise him for returning to you, gently cup the toy in one hand while offering a treat with the other hand. The **instant** your dog lets go of the toy you can say '**Drop**' or another chosen command word and offer the treat.*

gently cupping the toy with the other.
As he lets go say, '**Drop, good boy**' and **instantly** give the treat.

- Be prepared to exchange the toy for another if your dog is very toy-focused. Sometimes when they are in play-mode only a toy will do. Try the Fetch game with different toys and in different places.

- Practise for a few minutes and then change the game. A failure point in practising the retrieve comes when the dog has had enough and then refuses to return the toy, or won't run after it at all. Prevent this by halting the game before he is ready.

Below: Some dogs prefer to swap for another toy. If your puppy is reluctant to let go, stay relaxed. If you get impatient and tense, he will too which will make it less likely that he will let go.

The treat can be delivered when the toy has been released.

*Now you have the toy, **instantly** treat.*

Keep encouraging the return run so that he doesn't lose interest in the game.

Just wait and keep your voice soft and your face relaxed. Eventually he will let go and then you can reward him so that he will be keen to let go even more quickly next time.

TRAINING AT PLAY TIME!

To teach Shake A Paw, show your dog a treat in your closed fist.

*When he raises his paw to touch your hand, **instantly** 'click-treat'.*

*Give him the treat and then practise the trick again, perhaps adding the cue word '**Paw**'.*

We Know Tricks!

Here are some fun ideas if you have a few spare minutes and want some more structured trick-training, or something to teach your dog indoors. The following tricks can be taught in small spaces, while you watch TV, while the baby is asleep and even while you talk on the phone to a friend.

Shake A Paw

This is a fairly quick trick to teach. Dogs naturally lift paws in a gesture of appeasement and to signal 'play'.

- Sit in front of your dog holding a treat in your hand.
- Hold your closed fist at your dog's chest and allow him to sniff it.
- Eventually he is likely to raise a paw to try to get at the treat.
  - As he does, **instantly** 'click-treat' and reward him with the treat.
- Practise until he brings his paw up quickly each time.
- Then begin to say your verbal cue '**Paw**' as you perform the trick.

Above: This trick teaches your dog to raise his paw to touch your hand. With practice you can build the movement to resemble a wave.

Dance! Dance! Dance!

If your dog is physically suited to standing on his back legs you can teach him to 'dance'. You can do this while you wait for the kettle to boil or while taking a moment from your computer work.

- Tease your dog with a tasty treat or a toy and then raise it above his head so that he has to stand tall to reach it. **Instantly** '**click-treat**'.
- Slowly build up the time he has to stand upright before you 'click' and release the reward. Dogs need to move around a little in order to hold their balance.
- While he is upright say '**Dance**' and praise him. The more excited you are, the greater his enthusiasm for this game will be.
- Add in a spin or a twist by luring him around while he's in the '**Dance**' position. With practice you will be able to ask your dog to '**Dance**' and join you when you turn on your favourite music!

*'**Good boy**' for following the treat.*

*Above: You are looking for a raised posture in Dance! Dance! Dance!, so 'click-treat' the **instant** that your dog gets up on his hind legs.*

Encourage your dog to nose-touch the target stick when he's standing in front of you.

***Instantly** 'click-treat' the completed Bow before he's tempted into a Down position.*

Above left: A target stick allows you the luxury of teaching the Bow from the comfort of an armchair. No strenuous bending required.

Above right: Lower the target stick to the floor slowly. Your dog should follow it down with his nose and end up in a graceful bow.

Bow!

Teaching this trick is fairly easy because all dogs naturally use the play-bow position. You can use either a food lure or even have fun with a target stick.

- Encourage your dog into a **Stand** in front of you. Either hold a treat to his nose or use your target stick to influence his movements.
- Slowly move the lure downwards towards the spot so that your dog leans down to follow it. Within moments you should have a lovely bowing gesture.
- **Instantly** 'click-treat' or praise and reward. If you get your timing wrong he will probably sink into a full **Down** position instead.

A slight movement of the treat hand initiates a spin.

As the dog cranes his neck to follow the treat, he will naturally continue to spin around.

Above: As he gets more proficient at holding the position up on his hind legs, you can start to encourage him to spin around on his own axis.

Above: Eventually, if you have an agile dog, you should be able to entice him to perform a complete spin – or multiple spins – while he is standing on his hind legs. 'Click-treat' his successes.

TRAINING AT PLAY TIME!

His nose should follow the treat and his body will start to lean sideways.

You need to be quite precise with your hand movements – don't rush them.

Above: You begin to teach the roll-over with your dog in a conventional Down. Let him sniff the treat and then draw it back level with his shoulder.

Above: As you manoeuvre the treat round behind the dog's head, he will naturally have to roll onto his back if he is to keep it in sight.

Rollin' Rover

The roll-over can follow on nicely from the '**Down**' action and is suitable for dogs of any age as long as they are healthy. Very large breeds may find it harder to heave themselves over so you should make the judgement about your dog's physical ability.

- Begin with your dog in a **Down** position in front of you. Hold your treat to his nose and allow him to sniff. Slowly move your hand round to his shoulder so that he turns his head to follow it. If you go slowly enough, he should naturally shift his weight onto his shoulder. Release the treat once this stage is achieved.
- Repeat this stage until your dog is very comfortable shifting over onto his side. The next stage is to continue the lure further so that he rolls his whole body onto his back. **Instantly** 'click-treat' and praise

and reward your dog at this stage.
- Some dogs roll directly over from this position while others need you to continue the lure until they have completely rolled over. Break the movement down into as many parts as your dog requires.

Leg Weave

Teaching your dog to weave in and out of your legs is a fun game that can get you both into a bit of a tangle at first. The aim of this game is for your dog to weave in a figure-of-eight around your legs. The hand movements can be tricky to get right at first but soon your dog will be weaving through your legs with ease.

- Stand up with your legs apart. Hold a treat in each hand. Lure your dog through your legs from front to back using the treat in your right hand. As

Above: To teach the Weave you will need to equip yourself with a treat in each hand. In this way you can build up a fluent in-and-out motion.

Mark the completed roll-over with a 'click-treat'.

Above: 'Click-treat' initially as he rolls onto his back and then continue the movement so that he rolls right over. 'Click-treat' the finished trick.

Lend a hand with some extra legs!

Right: When your dog has mastered the basic weave through your legs, you can include another helper.

Above: Once your dog has made his way in and out of your legs successfully in a figure-of-eight pattern, **instantly** 'click-treat'.

your dog follows your hand through your legs, you should lure him around the outside of your right leg to the front. At this point you can offer the treat. Continue the weave by bringing your left hand behind your left leg and lure your dog back through your legs and round the outside towards the front again so completing the figure of eight. **Instantly** '**click-treat**' and offer your treat as he completes the move.

• Your command word may be '**Through**' or '**Weave**' and should be introduced once your dog is moving comfortably through your legs. Remember to praise your dog to keep the game fun. With practice you will be able to point and ask your dog to '**Weave**' without holding food in your hands.

• Once you have taught a basic leg weave you can extend this to include a stick or even another person. This is harder as you do not have both hands free to signal your dog to weave (unless you have a free-standing item to weave around). If you have a friend available to help, then ask them to stand in a line next to you with their legs apart. This trick requires team work and good timing by both trainers. Try not to ask for too many weaves without rewarding your dog at first or he may become tired of the game.

TRAINING AT PLAY TIME!

Armchair Training

Playtime doesn't have to end when you run out of energy and decide that it's time for a rest and perhaps a cup of tea in your armchair. The following pair of games make use of a chair both as a prop in the game and as a place where you can stretch out your legs to make an impromptu fence for your dog to jump over.

Hop Over

If your dog is mature and physically fit, you could teach him to jump even when you are sitting in an armchair and you don't want to get up and move around with him. This is much easier

Below: Begin to teach Hop Over by luring your dog to walk over your outstretched leg. Next speed this up so the dog starts to make a little hop, and then raise the height of your leg.

Above: A walking stick held low to the floor makes a nice easy jump for a very small dog.

with small to medium dogs as they can manoeuvre themselves in a smaller space.

- To get your dog used to the game, you can start by simply luring him to walk over your outstretched leg.
- As he learns the action and gains in confidence, encourage him to speed

up and actually make a little jump to clear the leg. **Instantly** 'click-treat' and praise and reward your dog when he is moving confidently over your leg.

- Once your dog is proving proficient at jumping over your leg as your foot rests on the floor, it is time to up the ante! Find a footstool or upturned wastepaper basket and rest your foot on that. Now you have quite a challenging hurdle for your dog to tackle.
- If you get tired of keeping your leg stretched out in front of you, you can use a walking stick or sturdy cane instead. This also has the advantage that you avoid the risks of bumps and bruises if the dog misjudges the jump. As with all jumping games, make sure that the take-off and landing areas are clear and not slippery.

Use the treat in your hand as the lure to tempt your dog over.

*'Click-treat' the **instant** that he makes a correct jump over your leg.*

As he gains confidence you can raise the bar.

Don't ask for too big a jump initially.

Your dog is enjoying active play while you are sitting down.

Above: This game encourages your dog to find a hidden treat or toy.

Find It

A 'Find it' game will encourage your dog to use his nose to provide him with stimulation and distraction. While gundogs will be especially good at this game, it is one that all breeds will be able to learn and enjoy to some level.

- A friend or family member should gently hold your dog by his collar or lead while you show him a favourite treat (or toy if preferred). Remain in sight while you place the treat under something easily moved such as a cushion.

- Your helper should then release your dog to run forwards to get the treat. If you don't have a helper, then try putting your dog behind a dog gate

A helper can hold the dog to prevent him from jumping the gun as you hide the treat.

Below: Once the treat has been hidden, the dog can be released to rush up and hunt for it behind the cushion.

He's keen to start looking for it.

*Below: When he noses it out, **instantly** click and say '**Find it**' while he enjoys his reward. Once he has got the hang of the game, you can increase the level of difficulty and make the treats harder to find.*

or attach his lead to something solid to keep him in place but still in view.

- He'll probably use his nose or paw to move the item hiding the treat. Say 'Find it' as he finds the treat and **instantly** 'click-treat' and praise and reward your dog at this stage. For more advanced dogs that know a reliable '**Stay**', use the command to keep them in place while you hide the lure, if you cannot call on the assistance of a helper.

- Keep practising by tucking treats behind chairs or in other safe locations within the room. Don't move to harder places until your dog can easily 'Find it' at this level.

GOOD HABITS: EVERYDAY TRAINING

That's Mine, Not Yours!

A common query that dog owners frequently ask me is how to stop their dog from taking the children's toys. The short answer is that it's probably unrealistic to expect that mistakes will not be made; lots of children's toys are pretty similar to dog toys and they often sound interesting and smell good (from children's sticky fingers or saliva).

When children see their teddy being paraded around the garden, it usually prompts an excited reaction and an urgent attempt to get the toy back. The dog is usually chased, shouted at, cornered, he loses the toy, then is often given a reprimand. Some, of course, are smacked too but remember that even pointing at or shaking a fist at your dog is threatening and scary, and counterproductive to good training.

How might your dog interpret this experience? He wanted to play and found something that he thought would be fun. After a while everyone suddenly reacted in a very shocking manner. Your dog probably won't associate this with the toy that he found minutes ago. First of all the chase may be fun and exciting for him which will encourage him to run around.

Above: If your dog runs away with a favourite possession, it's not a good idea simply to give chase. Ask him to bring it back to you – 'Fetch it' – and then try to swap it for one of his toys.

As people become more frustrated and cross, your dog will begin to feel worried and this is where problems occur. He will try to avoid you rather than bringing the toy to you. He will probably try to appease you as you come close. Remember that this is not an expression of guilt. Since you keep approaching and possibly remain angry, your dog may begin to react defensively. This is the start of many 'possessive' behavioural problems and is totally avoidable.

If you notice that your dog has picked up something that isn't his, **stay calm**. Practise your 'Fetch it' command to encourage him to approach and **swap** the item. Encourage him to play with his own toys. If he looks stressed, then walk away, giving him the space he needs to relax again. After a while call him over, or create a distraction instead.

Try to be really enthusiastic when your dog plays with his own toys. Don't take his engagement with them for granted. Otherwise he may pick up non-dog items to gain attention. The more you offer praise for him playing with the right items the more he will be drawn to these.

Below: To teach 'Leave it', first show your dog that you are holding a treat but do not let him have it.

Below: Tell him calmly to 'Leave it', and then wait until he stops showing signs of interest and turns away.

Below: Then instantly praise him and let him have a treat from your other hand. He gets the reward for ignoring the first treat item.

*Below: Once you have a reliable reaction to '**Leave it**', extend the training by hiding a treat under your foot.*

*Below: Again you are looking for the dog to respond to the '**Leave it**' command and turn his attention away from the treat back to you.*

*Below: When this happens, you are in a perfect position to reveal the treat reward **instantly** by simply lifting up your foot.*

'Leave it'

This command is extremely useful in many circumstances. You can reinforce it during regular training sessions that can be dotted throughout the day.

- Start by holding a treat or toy that your dog likes. Allow him to sniff at your hand but don't open it.
- Say '**Leave it**' in a calm, clear voice and wait until he turns away slightly. This may take a few moments.
  - **Instantly** praise him and offer another treat or toy from your other hand to reinforce his choice to move away from the original object of his attention.
- Practise this '**Leave it**' response until repeated success becomes really easy to achieve.

- Then try the same procedure with other items. With experience, your dog will start to generalise his response to whatever you are holding.
- Now try this command with an item under your foot.
- When this is successful try with items on the floor or coffee table. Always reward him for moving away. Remove the item after the session so he is not tempted to take it.
- Keep practising until he responds quickly and reliably no matter what item he has his attention focused on.

Instant Training Tip By avoiding the need to shout or chase your dog, he will have a more reliable response when you need him to leave something.

Below: The next stage of the training moves the tempting object away from your immediate person and onto a tabletop.

*Below: When you ask him to '**Leave it**', you want to see his focus move away from the cup containing treats and back to your face.*

*Below: Make sure that you have a treat concealed in your hand so that you can **instantly** reward compliance.*

GOOD HABITS: EVERYDAY TRAINING

Don't Disturb The Neighbours

Lots of dogs bark when they rush out into the garden. It is important that you prevent this from occurring straight away. Supervision is required at first but as your dog improves you will be able to relax also.

If your dog does start barking loudly when he goes outside, try to interrupt his behaviour by clapping your hands sharply and telling him to 'Leave it'.

Above: Ask your dog to 'Sit' before you take him out into the garden. A moment's control will help to prevent an outburst of excited barks.

- Keep a long line at the door so you can attach it each time your dog goes out.
- Ask your dog to 'Sit' while you open the door. If he jumps up to rush out, quickly close the door again. When he sits and waits nicely, 'click-treat'.
- Walk him out into the garden and then encourage him to go and toilet.
- While he remains quiet offer praise and intermittent 'click-treats'.
- As your training progresses you will

be able to offer the 'click-treat' for longer periods of quiet.

If he begins barking then
- Don't shout! Stay calm as this will have a better influence on your dog.
- Try to interrupt the noise of the barking by clapping loudly or asking him to 'Leave it'.
- If the barking continues, use the line to guide him gently back inside.

The consequences of being noisy are that your dog has to return indoors; being quiet extends his garden time. By avoiding chasing and exciting him you will have faster results.

Relaxing Around The Vacuum Cleaner

Many dogs chase or attack the vacuum. This may initially seem a hilarious game but it can soon turn into a difficult problem.

Take a few minutes before each cleaning session to begin training your dog to remain in his bed or to ignore the vacuum in the following way:
- Firstly never encourage your dog to chase brushes or vacuums. If you do, you are training him to do this and cannot complain if he doesn't stop when you decide that you've had enough.
- Position the vacuum in a room (switched off) and encourage your

Below: It's surprising how upset certain dogs get around a vacuum cleaner. Some seem to view it as a sort of prey animal and enjoy attacking the cleaning head, while others find the noise it makes quite alarming. The most extreme cases may develop a noise phobia related to the machine.

What starts like a game quickly turns into a serious nuisance.

The long extension pipes and flexible hose are exciting the terrier instinct in this little dog.

dog to enter. Ignore your dog if he approaches and sniffs it.
- Ask him to '**Sit**' in a position away from the vacuum. 'Click-treat' and praise him.

- Then move the vacuum a few inches. If your dog remains in place, then **instantly** 'click-treat' and toss a treat over to him. Repeat this several times, gradually building up the

movement of the vacuum. Always reinforce your dog's choice to remain sitting rather than getting up to attack the vacuum cleaner.
- After a few minutes end the session and encourage your dog to leave the room. You may wish to continue with your genuine cleaning at this time.
- The next step is to switch the vacuum on. Avoid doing this close to your dog. 'Click' and treat him for sitting and not moving towards the vacuum cleaner.
- Gradually build up some movement so that his tolerance increases. Try not to vacuum towards your dog and never pen him into a corner.
- If your dog has a bad chase problem or is overly sensitive to noises, then you should always shut him in another room or the garden while you are vacuuming your home.

The aim is to bring the machine gradually closer and then turn it on while he sits in his bed.

Instantly 'click-treat' and reward good behaviour.

Above: Begin to accustom your dog to the vacuum cleaner by making him sit quietly while it is also in the room, initially switched off.

Above: As you manoeuvre the cleaner nearer to the dog, keep 'click-treating' and tossing rewards to him if he remains sitting on his bed.

Above: Bit by bit the dog should get used to the sound and, eventually, the movement of the vacuum in his presence.

CHAPTER 10

TRAINING FOR WHEN VISITORS CALL

Guests Arriving

It is an understandably exciting time for most dogs when people come to call at the house. You can improve your dog's responses by following some consistent training every time someone arrives at your door. Even if your dog is genuinely happy to see the person, his behaviour may be worrying to your visitor.

If your dog has ever been aggressive towards people, then it may be sensible to encourage him into another room before you open the door. This allows you to avoid problems as the person enters. Controlled meetings with helpers is a sensible way to approach this problem.

For friendly, yet exuberant, dogs you should train your dog to respond more appropriately.

- Begin training without anyone at the door.
- Pick a place where you would like your dog to sit while guests enter. Make sure there is space to open the door and for people to enter.
- Practise asking him to '**Sit**' and '**Stay**' in this spot while you 'click-treat' good responses.
- Gradually approach the door, 'click-treating' your dog for remaining in position. Practise until you can approach and open the door without your dog getting up.
- Now you can ask a family member or helper to knock or ring the bell while you practise. On hearing the sound proceed exactly as you have been practising with your 'click-treat' routine. It may take a lot of practice before you can open the door since the sound of the knocker or bell will probably excite your dog.
- If your dog jumps up, close the door and wait quietly until he turns his focus on you again. When he does, encourage him onto his spot and **instantly** 'click-treat'. He will eventually learn that this is the correct response when he hears the doorbell or knocker.

- Build up to being able to open the door with your helper standing outside. If your dog gets up, close the door immediately and re-start the attempted introduction.
- You may wish to attach a houseline to his collar to reduce the possibility of your dog managing to escape through the door.
- If your dog cannot resist getting up as the person enters the home, you may have to maintain eye contact with him as they enter so he remains focused upon you. Try to pre-empt his attempts to move towards your guest by stepping in front of him and getting his attention back on you again.
- With regular practice your dog should learn to be very polite when your guests enter.

No harassment Friendly dogs often pester guests who may not appreciate their presence in the same way that you do. If your dog likes to jump all over your guests, attach a houseline to his collar and use this to prevent him from doing so. 'Click-treat' when your dog does not jump and follows your 'sit to greet' routine.

Instant Training Tip: Try to keep an interesting chew or activity toy to offer your dog when guests visit. Your dog will benefit as something nice always happens when guests visit and your guest will benefit from avoiding being jumped on or licked.

Right: Make sure that any introductions to children are monitored by yourself or another adult.

Initially you may just approach and open the door while there is no-one there. If that goes well, ask a friend to act as a visitor.

If guests are staying over, perhaps during holiday periods, then remember that this puts more pressure onto your dog so ensure that he can still move away and find quiet time and space whenever he needs it. Create a safe den area to which he can retreat for peace and quiet. Guests should be advised never to disturb him in this place. Select a quiet place where he can go whenever he feels the need.

*Left: It may take several attempts before your dog will accept you opening the door and a visitor coming into the room without moving from his **Sit**. Use your 'click-treats' to reward him.*

*Above: If your dog gets very excited when guests arrive, perhaps jumping up at them in an unwelcome way, you have to gradually train him to remain in a quiet **Sit** when there is a knock on the door or ring of the bell.*

He hasn't moved from his spot, so he fully deserves a 'click-treat'.

Meeting Children

Make sure that any children are seated on a chair or down on the floor before you let your dog approach them. Small children should be seated either on an adult's knee or next to them. Practise asking your dog to '**Sit**' while they treat and stroke him. If he is likely to snatch at the treats, then it may be better not to use these. Watch your dog closely and call him away if you observe any signs of stress.

*Right: Make sure the treat comes the **instant** that you 'click' good behaviour. The dog will learn that a steady **Sit** brings nice rewards.*

CHAPTER 11

TRAINING AT MEALTIMES

Relaxing Around The Dog Bowl

Aggression shown by a dog around a food bowl *(right)* is a far too common and unnecessary canine problem. By the time the dog is showing aggression, it is likely that he has being feeling stressed for some time. By being aware of your dog's body language you are less likely to find this situation developing in your house.

Aggression indicates that your dog believes that this resource may be taken away from him and so he feels that he has to protect it. Try not to label him 'dominant' at this stage since it's more likely that he's anxious. Therefore you need to teach him that people passing by or approaching are nothing to worry about. Before we see actual aggression, we often see warning signs, such as the puppy or dog standing over the bowl, going still, stopping wagging his tail, licking his lips or lowering his head over the bowl without eating. If this happens when you are around, then you need to work on this situation immediately.

The aim should be to teach your dog to relax when you're near. Clearly this does not replace the sensible advice that children should always stay away from the dog while he is

Before we see actual aggression we often see warning signs

eating. If it is not already on there, then add this to your House Rules list straight away.

First of all don't think that taking the food bowl away to show your dog who's boss is going to help. This will only stress him further. Every member of the pack needs to eat and is entitled to protect the resources they have.

Prepare a food container with varied treats and place this on the counter in your kitchen or near to where your dog eats. Every time you come into the room you should **instantly** take a treat from the tub and toss it into the bowl. When your dog is eating his dinner you can also do this. Don't approach too closely or try to interact; the aim is to appear totally relaxed and non-threatening. Casually take a treat, toss it onto/near to the bowl and continue with your routine. If you intend to stay in the room, then take a few more pieces and offer those intermittently before you leave.

Below: To help your dog relax around his bowl, casually pick up a few treats when you enter the kitchen.

This dog is guarding his bowl.

Below: Throw the treats down in or around the food bowl and move on. You don't have to make eye contact or engage with your dog; just act nonchalantly.

Below: As your dog becomes more relaxed about your presence around his bowl, you'll be able to come closer to it before you dispense the next handful of treats.

After a while your dog will learn that your presence means that nice things arrive in the bowl, so it is better not to chase you away.

Gradually as your dog learns to anticipate the arrival of the tasty reward, you can start to take a step towards the bowl before throwing the treat and walking away. Eventually you will be able to approach close to your dog while he is eating. If your dog is relaxed, he will show happy body language, a swooshing tail wag and no longer display any tension or stress signals.

Instant Training Tip If your dog has been showing severe aggression around food for a long time, then please seek personal behavioural support from a canine behaviourist as this training task is more challenging and should be broken down into a much slower, more comprehensive guide designed specifically for your case.

No Begging

Most of us dislike a dog that sits staring and drooling while we eat. Despite this many dogs are encouraged to do this by being offered titbits from our plates or table. We often think, 'What harm can it do now and again?' Even occasional success will keep your dog begging for a long time so everyone

Left: This process of gradually accustoming the dog to your proximity to his bowl, and the fact that you come bearing gifts, should eventually make the problem disappear. You no longer seem to threaten his food resource.

Left: Don't tolerate begging. Teach your dog to stay on his bed, perhaps with a food-stuffed toy, while you enjoy a snack or a meal.

should try to follow the same rules with this one. Otherwise you should accept that your dog will always try to see what's on offer.

You have different options depending upon your circumstances. Firstly you could choose to put your dog into another room while you eat. This is a particularly good idea if you have young children who cannot follow your rules about not offering food to the dog. It is also a very quick method to dispel begging behaviour.

- Alternatively, teach your dog to lie down on his bed while you eat. You will need to practise sending him to his bed so that he already understands this command.
- Practise so that he is familiar with you sitting at the table while he sits or lies on his bed. Get up and approach him to 'click-treat' (rather than throwing treats from the table).
- Practise eating snacks at the table first and build up to a full meal. While you eat continue to reinforce him for staying in his bed by praising him.
- It will help to give him something of his own to occupy him during this tempting time. A stuffed activity toy is a great way to keep his nose away from your food.

It looks cute but it can lead to an annoying habit of begging.

Right: Take care that you maintain the distinction between using food treats in training and indiscriminately indulging a dog that begs for food from the table. The latter behaviour can become a serious nuisance.

CHAPTER 12

END OF THE DAY

So you've sat down in your chair to try to relax and catch up on some television or conversation with your family. What is your dog doing? Did you know that you could even be training him at this time? Lots of owners ban their dog from the living area because they won't settle or they get into mischief. Remember that without practice your dog is likely to be over-excited at this time and is more likely to make mistakes. So, although it may mean improving your own multi-tasking skills, you can work on training your dog even while you are sitting down and relaxing.

You can work on training your dog even while you are sitting down and relaxing

'Off The Chair'

Perhaps your dog has beaten you to it. How you react depends upon your house rules as you may be happy for your dog to be on there at any time. If not, try not to shout at your dog or he may learn to become defensive as you approach. Instead, **instantly** create a distraction, such as by clapping your hands, to encourage your dog to get off the sofa. As he does, give your '**Off**' command and praise him. He will learn that '**Off**' is a good command. If you avoid confrontation he'll have no need to resist.

'Settle'

Do you expect your dog to lie down quietly while you are watching your favourite show? Unless you have taught him to do this, he will probably make a mistake. Position his bed or a blanket near your feet. Bring him into the room with his lead clipped to his collar and take your seat. Ask him to lie down on his blanket. As soon as he does, be prepared **instantly** to 'click-treat' and/or praise him. Offer him a chewy or a stuffed activity toy so that he has something to do. When he is lying quietly introduce your cue word '**Settle**' and praise him.

If you're using your clicker, then click frequently and toss the treat onto his bed so that he does not need to get up and break the '**Settle**'.

You will need to do this consistently each night to see improvement. Gradually build up the time he has to lie quietly. At the end of each session give your release command and then encourage him to move through to an area where you normally leave him for the night, probably where his bed is, or even into a dog crate. If time allows, you can try to fit in another session that same evening. If your dog has spent a lot of time alone during the day, then you need to make every effort to ensure he can spend time with you during the evenings. If you take him for a really good walk before attempting this command you will find it easier to get him to

Encourage him rather than shouting a reprimand.

The chair is vacant; job done.

Above: If you don't want your dog to share your chairs, make sure that you command him to get down whenever he is on one.

*Above: Give your '**Off**' command as he jumps down and praise and treat him. It's fun to get down when rewards are around.*

'Click-treat' intermittently to reward a prolonged period of quietness.

The treat arrives right after the 'click'.

Above: You can even fit in a bit of training when you are relaxing at the end of the day; this exercise teaches the dog to settle on his bed.

Above: When he is lying quietly, say '**Settle**' and 'click-treat' him. If the bed is some way away, throw the treat rather than making him move.

Above: At then end of the session, give a release command, treat again and prepare your dog for lights out.

relax. If you put the effort in, your dog should be able to spend more and more time with you each day without becoming a pest, which will benefit you both.

The Dog Bed

Position your dog's bed in a quiet location, away from direct human traffic. He should feel safe when he goes to this place and able to relax in the knowledge that he can rest completely. Ideally the bed should be away from draughts and the area should be dark. Some dogs like to have blankets to bury underneath. Do not allow your children to sit in the bed, or to jump in with your dog. If he is trying to rest but cannot get away from them, he may become irritable. A dog gate is extremely useful in providing an area that is reliably secure from young children. Your dog can rest completely in the knowledge that he won't be woken.

Bed Time

Many dogs get tired in the evenings and may become aggressive if they are disturbed. An easy way to reduce the likelihood of this is to decide on a bedtime for your dog, prior to the time when he is most sleepy and irritable. Once he has been put to bed, don't go in to kiss goodnight or disturb him without very good reason. Think about how grumpy you would be if you were constantly being woken up. If you need your dog try to call him out of his bed or arouse him verbally before you approach and touch him since doing so unannounced could cause him alarm.

End of the Day

As bedtime beckons you can probably think of many ways in which your dog has been exposed to instant training opportunities during the course of the day. And

you can probably think of ways in which you need to improve your training and areas where your dog needs some extra work. As each day passes you will progress towards your aim. You should now restock the treat tubs and reposition the dog toys in strategic places so you will always have one to hand when tomorrow dawns. Set your alarm now if your dog has a toilet training problem and needs to go out early. Remember that your training efforts will have the desired results if you are prepared and ready always to encourage the right responses **instantly**!

INDEX

Page references set in **bold** type indicate a main entry; *italics* indicate an illustration.

INSTANT DOG TRAINING

Picture Credits

Unless otherwise credited below, all the photographs in this book were taken by Roddy Paine and are © Interpet Publishing Ltd. Positions on the page are abbreviated as follows: top (t), left (l), right (r), centre (c), bottom (b).

Jane Burton, Warren Photographic: 19c, 21cr.

Dreamstime.com Nivi: 11tl.

Fotolia.com biglama: 31cl. CallallooAlexis: 70tr. cynoclub: 18cl, 36bl. Dagel: 46tc. Dngood: 31tr. EastWest Imaging: 12tr. Barbara Helgason: 4tl, 71b. Min McCann: 69t. www.glanzbilder.org: 5br, 58cl, 60cl.

Interpet Archive: 18tl, 19br, 27b sequence, 28 sequence, 30tc, 30c, 32tc, 32c sequence, 33tl, 55cl, 60 headcollar and harness, 62tc, 62b.

iStockphoto.com Joachim Angeltun: 89t door. Anyka: 54tl. Emmanuelle Bonzami: 13cl. Carrie Bottomley: 35bl. Dan Brandenburg: 12cl. Jani Bryson: 20br. Robert Carner: Back cover bc, 34tr. Henri Caroline: 17tl. Andraz Cerar: 31tc. Anne Clark: 9br. Andy Cook: Instant timer artwork. craftvision: 73t. Hanna Monika Cybulko: 21br. Donald Erikson: 26c. Wojciech Gajda: 9tl. Stacey Gamez: 34cl. Hedda Gjerpen: 63tl, 64cl. Steve Goodwin: 14tc. Jen Grantham: 25tl, 26cl, 39bc. Kim Gunkel: 70bl. Konstantin Gushcha: 93cr. Drew Hadley: 22tc. Kirby Hamilton: Front cover stopwatch, 1, 2, 4 and 6 stopwatch. HannamariaH: 35br, 75bl. happyborder: 14br. Geoff Hardy: 17bc. Mark Herreid: 70br. Gregory Horler: 17c. Waltraud Ingerl: 4cl, 75tr. Eric Isselée: 10tl, 10 cr, 16 main image, 16cl, 17tc, 17cl, 19 Dalmatian tail, 19 Airedale tail, 35t, 36br, 38tc, 40bc, 42tc, 44tc, 48tc, 90t dog. Kamo: 64tr. Anna Khomulo: 9cl. Peter Kirillov: 6bl. kkymek: 37cl. Natalia Kuznetsova: 15br. lendry: 63br. Michelle Levante: 18tc. Tomaz Levstek: 18-19. Li Kim Goh: 25tr. Erik Lam: 86tl, Lesley Lister: 5 tr, 88t. Warwick Lister-Kaye: 10bc. Pamela Moore: 37br, 74bl. Kati Neudert: 53tc. Brian Palmer: 16bl. Joanna Pecha: 24br. pederk: 16c. PhotoTalk: 47cr. Andrejs Pidjass: 21bl. PK-Photos: 15tl. Nikolay Pozdeev: 91br. rambo182: 51 door. redmal: 90t bowl. Frans Rombout: 76tl. ranplett: 24bl. Nell Redmond: 20cl. Martti Slamela: 53cr. Sarah Salmela: 16tc, 16tr, 74cr. Leigh Schindler: 37tc. Angelika Schwarz: Front cover bl. Michael Skelton: 51cr. Spectral-Design: 86t door. Mike Sonnenberg: 40tc. Alexey Stiop: 8tr, 35c. Lisa Svara: 18bc. Pavel Timofayev: 38bl, 38br. Vitaly Titov: 56tc. Nikolai Tsvetkov: 14cl. walik: 21tl. Lauri Wiberg: 23b. WilleeCole: 36tr. Monika Wisniewska: 5cr.

PetSTEP Inc.: 63tr.

Shutterstock Inc. Eric Isselée: 51tr.

Acknowledgements

Thanks to all the people who've been involved in the production and development of this book at all stages. A big thank you to animal handler, Sue Ottmann, for helping out so well at the photoshoots and for helping to gather together such lovely owners and dogs. I'd like to thank my husband Ross for once again supporting me and tolerating my late night typing and say thank you to Ruth Nicholls who gave up her time to proof-read my text and offer her useful comments.

I'm extremely grateful to all the owners who gave their time and lent us their well-behaved dogs for photography: Serena-Lily Hancock and Maisy, Hayley Merrick and Dave, Katie Simpson and Brogan and Echo, Alison Smith and Oscar. It was lovely working with you.

The Author

Claire Arrowsmith is the principal consultant at The Pet Behaviour Centre running clinics across a wide area including the Queen's Veterinary School Cambridge. She is a full member of the Association of Pet Behaviour Counsellors (APBC) and holds an Honours degree in Zoology and a Masters degree in Applied Animal Behaviour and Animal Welfare. Claire has been working as a behaviour consultant for ten years and has worked with rescue animals and Hearing Dogs for Deaf People.

Claire features in her own 'Puppy Training', 'Trick Training' and 'Banishing Bad Behaviour' DVDs by Houndstar Films and features on the expert panel of Your Dog magazine providing answers to readers' questions. She is the author of *Brain Games For Dogs, Correcting Bad Habits In Dogs, The Sit, Down, Come, Heel, Stay and Stand Book, The Kitten Pack* and *What If My Cat...?*.

Claire lives with her husband and their rescue Rhodesian Ridgeback mix dog, Sarnie, their two naughty cats, Pickle and Lenny, and their three even naughtier hens, Olive, Betty and Beryl.